I'll Drop You a Line

I'll Drop You a Line

A Life with David Marcus

ITA DALY

LONDUBH

First published in 2016

Londubh Books
18 Casimir Avenue, Harold's Cross, Dublin 6w, Ireland
www.londubh.ie

1 3 5 4 2

Origination by Londubh Books; cover by Bluett
Printed by ScandBook AB, Falun, Sweden
ISBN: 978-1-907535-80-2

A Note on the Text
The text is set in Adobe Garamond Pro.
Chapter headings are set in Forum.

For Sarah

I'll Drop You a Line

– One –

When people talk of the 1960s they seem to recall a decade of change and excitement, of youth culture, the miniskirt and the Beatles: to be young was very heaven then, or so one might be led to believe. Not for me, a twenty-something-year-old living in Dublin, a small, tight, provincial city, hardly changed from the place James Joyce had written about half a century earlier.

Maybe it was even less urban than Joyce's city for, in the intervening years, with the expansion of the civil service and the building of more schools and hospitals, it had been flooded with the sons and daughters of farmers and shopkeepers from every county in Ireland. It was a capital city that reflected the country – white, Catholic and conservative. The city was ruled from the archbishop's palace in Drumcondra rather than City Hall and the Protestant university – Trinity College – was forbidden to Catholics by edict of Archbishop John Charles McQuaid.

I remember attending a science conference organised by the universities for second-level students when I was in fifth year in school. All those who attended were issued with lunch vouchers, some for University College, Dublin, others for Trinity. Before the end of the morning session an announcement was made: any Catholic student who had been issued with a voucher for Trinity was to ignore this and instead head for Newman House, where, presumably, the beef and carrots would be Catholic. This was the level of segregation that existed in Dublin and I don't think

Protestants wanted to mix with us any more than we wanted to mix with them. Protestants had their own tennis clubs and golf clubs and kept themselves to themselves. I had a Methodist boyfriend who told me that when he started university his grandmother had made him promise to eschew the demon drink and Roman Catholic girlfriends.

Almost everyone in Dublin was Irish: there were only a few brown or black students, no Eastern Europeans and very few people from western Europe: no debates about what we should call the New Irish because there were only the Old Irish. There was, however, among this homogeneous mass, a tiny minority, unnoticed for the most part because of its low profile and statistical unimportance – I am talking about the Jews.

At the time I'm referring to the Jews were our only recent immigrants. Most of them arrived towards the end of the 19th century, settling in Dublin, Limerick and Cork. The wandering Jew has never wanted to assimilate. He has kept himself to himself, anxious to hold on to his identity, living within walking distance of a synagogue, moving in a community that not only has its own schools and clubs but its own kosher shops. The only meaningful assimilation of Jews that ever took place was in Germany and Austria before the Second World War, a horrible irony.

Because we Irish were never threatened by waves of immigrants and because it was already a segregated society, the Jews had no difficulty in fitting in, as long as they kept their heads down and worked hard – which, on the whole, they did. Most people wouldn't have known any Jews and the only time they were likely to be reminded of their existence was on Good Friday, as that day's liturgy enjoined them to 'pray for the perfidious Jews'.

So it is hardly surprising that, when I told my parents I intended to marry a Jew, their first reaction was not to seek out the dusty bottle of Harvey's Bristol Cream to toast the happy couple.

A Jew? Where had I even found one?

There are hardly any Jews left in Ireland now and this is

Ireland's loss. For many years they enriched our lives, as immigrants normally enrich the lives of the host community. This was especially true of the family of David Marcus, the man I intended to marry. Long before I met David, my father used to talk about a remarkable solicitor in Cork, a champion of the poor and the underdog. This was Gerald Goldberg, David's maternal grandfather. He must have been a bit of a legend if my father had heard of him.

His son, David Goldberg, is an original and talented painter. The youngest member of the Marcus family, Louis, has had a long and distinguished career as a film-maker, winning many awards along the way. In recent years he has begun painting and regularly shows at the RHA annual exhibition. Two of his sons have also contributed to the arts, Daniel as a musician and Shimmy as a film-maker. Another cousin, the late Louis Lentin, was a gifted television and film director and David's sister, Nella, had a brilliant career in the Artists and Repertoire Department of Decca Records, where she looked after the careers of singers like Joan Sutherland and Luciano Pavarotti

Their contribution to the arts is especially interesting because it is so much at variance with the story of the money-grubbing Jew. If one wants to get rich quick, if one wants to get rich at all, one eschews the arts. It is remarkable, then, that so many of this family not only had the talent to pursue artistic careers but the courage to do so. In the 1940s and 1950s, before the era of Arts Council funding, most artists didn't give up the day job but David's brother Louis never had a day job and David abandoned the Bar after a year. This suggests to me parents who had an extraordinary belief in their children and, more unusually, a profound respect for the arts.

With debates on immigration raging all over Europe I often think how lucky it was for Ireland that, some time in the 1880s, the Marcus and Goldberg families washed up on our shores.

– Two –

I met David when I submitted a short story to the New Irish Writing page which he had not long before established in the *Irish Press*. I had never had anything published and I was delighted when, about three weeks after I sent in my story, I had a letter from David asking me to come in to discuss it.

The *Irish Press*, founded by Éamon de Valera, was going through a golden era under the editorship of Tim Pat Coogan, who had set about transforming a dullish, partisan news sheet into a vibrant, intelligent newspaper, hiring young journalists like Mary Kenny and making room for one whole page every week to be devoted to Irish writing – poetry and fiction – without any advertisements.

New Irish Writing was a phenomenon that changed the face of contemporary writing in Ireland and it came about because of David's courage and devotion. In his career path we can see a consistency: he took chances and welcomed change. He had trained as a barrister but, finding that the law was indeed an ass, abandoned his career after a year and returned to his first love by starting up a literary magazine which he cheekily called *Irish Writing*.

This was in the 1940s, the heyday of the literary magazine, but even so it took some chutzpah for a twenty-two-year-old with no literary connections to embark on such a project. Perhaps it helped that he was living in Cork, home to two of our most talented and successful short story writers, Frank O'Connor and Sean O'Faolain.

By 1956 the magazine had folded and David, now with debts to be cleared, headed for London. Although he already had three siblings living there and his parents were to follow eventually, he never really settled and in 1969, encouraged by his brother Louis – still living in Ireland – he returned to his native land, not to Cork but to Dublin, where he had neither job nor contacts. He kept himself going, initially, by submitting bits and pieces of journalism to Seán McCann, who was Features Editor of the *Evening Press*; what he really wanted, though, was to get back to the business of finding and publishing new writers. Very quickly he came up with an audacious idea. He would not start a literary magazine – been there, done that – but how about trying to persuade some newspaper editor to include a short story in his paper every week? This was a completely original idea, simple and brilliant in its concept. Unlike literary magazines, newspapers have a readership of tens of thousands. These readers would now be getting a weekly short story at no extra cost and the writers would have a potential readership beyond their most optimistic imaginings.

The obvious newspaper to which to take the idea was *The Irish Times* and David was on his way there when he called in to the Silver Swan pub to have a coffee with Seán McCann. When he told Seán what he intended, Seán said, 'No, take it to Tim Pat. I'm sure he'll run with the idea.'

Thus did New Irish Writing find its first home.

– Three –

I had been writing since I was twelve, stories and longer pieces, all abandoned before they were finished. I had even gone to a creative writing course – although it wasn't called that – when I answered a small advertisement in the *Evening Press*. It was one of the strangest experiences of my life.

At this time creative writing courses really took place only in American universities and maybe that is where our mentor got his idea. He was a chain smoker in his fifties and held the classes in his dank flat on Adelaide Road. There were four of us aspiring writers – me, an elderly Anglo-Irish woman and two men in their twenties, one of whom was writing a particularly bloody thriller which he insisted on reading to us with glee.

I think our tutor was English and he may have had something published in the 1930s but that is all any of us knew about him. He didn't talk very much, merely nodding now and then as he puffed on his roll-ups. He appeared to me to be deeply depressed and this, combined with the dankness of the room in which we gathered, seemed to give an air of authenticity to the proceedings. Occasionally, our mentor did utter an arcane comment but mainly it was a battle of egos among the writers to have their work heard.

The thriller writer was hard to shut up and the other young man spent most of his time staring at his boots, every now and again querulously squeaking a comment. The Anglo-Irish woman, timid but persistent, wanted to write about what she described as 'sadly, a dying world' and I didn't know what I wanted to write about.

I went to the class two or three times and found its usefulness lay in getting me motivated. Listening to the others gave me the impetus to get down to work and soon, although I stopped going to the class, I finished a short story.

But I was young and fickle, with many other things on my mind. I put the story in a drawer and forgot all about it. Then I met a man and fell in love and was duly dumped. When I had recovered from my broken heart, true to the cliché, I sought revenge – a literary revenge: I would write a story about what had happened but in the story *I* would do the dumping.

That story wrote itself and I wanted it to be published. Try New Irish Writing, someone suggested. We didn't subscribe to the *Irish Press* at home so I had never seen the page but when I got a copy I discovered that there was an invitation from the editor for writers to send in a story or poem. You didn't need to have been published; all you had to do was send a stamped addressed envelope with your submission and the editor would read your story and consider it for publication.

The page, I was later to learn, also published stories by established, even famous Irish authors. Writers like William Trevor and Edna O'Brien appeared there. Their story would not be an unpublished one, of course – the *Irish Press* couldn't have afforded such fees – but earlier publication in the *New Yorker* or some other American or English literary magazine meant that, in reality, the story was new for most Irish readers. The big names added lustre to the page and David's way of getting them was an example of his clever, dextrous thinking. He never worried about problems; he solved them.

I read my letter from David Marcus three times, then rang up and made an appointment to come in and see him, as I had been invited to do.

I arrived into the front office, all dressed up in my fun fur, and waited at the desk for David to descend from his eyrie, a small room right at the top of the building. I was already nervous and I was further intimidated by the formality of his greeting. As a friend said at his funeral, David had the manners of an Edwardian gentleman. After we shook hands he suggested that we go around the corner to the Silver Swan to talk about the story or, as he put it, 'to discuss your work'.

This phrase made me feel like a real writer but an increasingly nervous one and when David asked me what I would like – meaning tea or coffee – I looked around the almost empty pub and wondered how I could get through the next half-hour. I would be discovered. I wouldn't be able to talk about literature or say anything intelligent.

In desperation I said, 'I'll have a double Jameson.' Writers were serious hard-drinking people and, besides, I needed some Dutch courage. It was eleven in the morning but I was a writer.

To give him his due, my future husband didn't flinch.

David's love affair with the short story had begun long before we met and continued throughout our married life and until the day he died. In his late teens he had read William Saroyan's collection, *The Daring Young Man on the Flying Trapeze*, and fallen in love with the form. He read short stories, he wrote them and eventually he devoted his life to helping thousands of them, conceived by other writers, through the birth canal. His tiny office on Burgh Quay was the maternity ward where he combined the roles of obstetrician and midwife, reading every manuscript that came into him, working on it with the author, seeing talent in imperfect stories where other editors might have seen only flaws.

David told me straight away that the story I had submitted was not going to be published but that he thought I had talent. He suggested that I go home and write another story and send it to him. He told me to put the original story away and come back to it later on as it might be easier at this stage to embark on something new.

Any disappointment I felt was outweighed by my excitement. I had talent: what more can any young writer hope to hear? I also learned from that first meeting that writing is hard work. David explained that by a fluke a story, often a first story, will write itself but this seldom happens and if one wants to become a professional writer one must be prepared for the everyday dullness that goes with any job. There was no point in hanging around waiting for inspiration to strike because one might wait for ever. The thing to do was to sit down at a particular hour every day and try to produce something. You might sit there for a week and nothing will emerge but something will eventually happen provided you put in the work.

Now that creative writing courses have become commonplace, I imagine every young writer knows this but when David started his New Irish Writing page, this sort of advice and encouragement was not readily available. You sent a story to one or other of the magazines that published short stories and if you were lucky you got a rejection slip. More often, the story disappeared into the ether and was never seen again. I sympathise with the editors of these magazines. We are a nation of writers and would-be writers; everyone has a book in them or, at the very least, a story. Most magazine editors soon found themselves fighting for breath under an ever-growing heap of submissions.

The reason David could cope so well was that his was an exclusive devotion. He had few distractions. Principally, as a non-drinker he didn't spend time in pubs, which in the 1970s played a large part in most people's lives. In those days you could divide people into the drinkers and dreamers who whiled away the hours in pubs and lounges and the doers who were usually teetotal and organised and ran amateur Ireland, from the dramatic and musical societies to the GAA. David established the New Irish Writing page, breathing life into the short story and giving a platform to a whole generation of new writers. There was nothing amateur about his undertaking but being wifeless, childless and almost friendless as well as a non-drinker he had the necessary time to become something unique: an editor who read your story with care and gave you a considered answer promptly.

When I met him he was devoting his life to this project. He was a man of few needs and little ego. He was indifferent to or, more accurately, unaware of public opinion. He had come back from London to live in Dublin, a bachelor in his mid-forties and set in his ways, knowing nobody except his brother. I think he might have remained thus, contented and solitary, if I hadn't wandered into his life that spring morning.

I say contented rather than happy. He was glad to be back in Ireland, really glad to be doing work that mattered so much to him but, apart from that, his life was pretty bleak. Every evening he returned from work, his briefcase heavy with manuscripts. En route he would stop off at the supermarket to buy a tin of salmon or half a dozen eggs, ingredients for a simple evening meal that he would cook in his tiny kitchenette. He would read the stories and poems that he had brought home and, later on, listen to music until it was bedtime.

On Friday he would go to Louis and his wife, Chookie, for Shabbat supper; otherwise he rarely went out. He was isolated, even more than he had been in London, but he was stoical and when I got a glimpse into this life for the first time I know that it upset me far more than it seemed to be upsetting him. He had learned acceptance.

I tried to make sense of him as I began to get to know him. His habits and desires were so different from mine: as well as being teetotal he had no interest in food. He didn't know the meaning of indulgence, never lingering in bed, never snacking and drinking coffee or tea only when he was thirsty. He didn't drive or smoke and although he did back horses that was more a passion than an indulgence. This makes him sound austere but austerity is a question of temperament. It wasn't that David was denying himself anything; he just didn't seem to need these things. I found this really hard to understand because along with this monk-like existence went a passionate temperament. His greatest passion, even maybe surpassing his love of the short story, was for music. He had a large collection of tapes which he listened to every day as well as listening to BBC Radio 3. He played the piano but, believing himself to be no good, never played in front of anyone. If someone came into the room he immediately stopped. However, after we were married the sound of his playing behind a closed door became the musical accompaniment of my life. He only ever played the same Mozart concerto, not in its entirety, just the first few bars. These he went over again and again, starting at the beginning each time he played a wrong note. I don't know if he could play anything else or why he never tried; I just accepted it as a quirk. Looking back now, it seems very strange, an indication, perhaps, of his intolerance of the mediocre. 'Ah sure it'll be grand' was not an approach that David entertained.

His most singular characteristic and the thing I envied most was the fact that he was always himself, no matter in whose company or whatever the circumstances. This is something that can be said about very few people and I see it as a sort of gift.

These are things I learned about David in the course of our life together. That we got together at all was due to David's persistence and confidence for, although he was diffident, if he really wanted something he went after it and didn't give up.

After that first meeting and I had had a story accepted we started going out together. Initially, I didn't see it in this light for I really only saw him in relation to my work. With his praise I began to think that maybe I could write and I started taking the whole thing seriously. When David asked me out to dinner, he may have seen it as a date but I saw it more as a workshop. We talked about writing and I listened, eager for any advice he could offer. I wasn't looking for romance: I had left that behind with my broken heart.

But romance developed – and quite quickly. I think that he had fallen in love with me straight away and after a few meetings, although slow on the uptake, I began to notice this. I saw how he looked at me and I knew that it wasn't jut as one of his writers; this, inevitably, led to my viewing him in a different light. I saw that this mentor, this man, was very attractive – diffident but at the same time sure of what he wanted.

Falling in love is all about sex. If the relationship develops, other aspects of it will develop too but if that sexual charge is not there right from the beginning nothing can happen. When I stopped to look I knew that it was definitely present in our relationship.

So our meetings became dates for me too and soon, without pretence on either side, we were going to the theatre regularly or out to dinner in the old Unicorn Restaurant on Merrion Row or the Trocadero, a very different restaurant then from what it later became.

As a suitor David had a lot going for him. For a start he liked women, something that is not at all a given. Then he had such delightful, old-fashioned manners that sort of wrapped around me, making me feel special and cherished. I know it goes against everything liberated young women are expected to feel but I liked the fact that, in restaurants, after we had chosen what we wanted to eat, he did the ordering. I liked the fact that he stood up when I came into a room and that he always walked on the outside on a pavement. I felt that I was protected but never for a moment did I feel that I wasn't David's equal and neither did he. This was why I could enjoy the old-fashioned courtesy: there was nothing condescending about it.

He was also a skilful ballroom dancer. I was just too late to have learned this skill, being part of the new dawn of shufflers who thought it was cool to throw their arms around a bit and move their feet and dance parallel to their partner. People who haven't experienced ballroom dancing don't know what an aphrodisiac it is. The music is romantic, the mood is set, the rhythm carries you away as two bodies bend and blend. David, normally so diffident, became masterful on the dance floor and I stumbled after him with delight.

He was nineteen years older than me but this made him all the more attractive. I was used to boys who weren't sure of themselves or the new role that had been assigned to them in the whole dating, mating game. David seemed polished and knew what to do; he had been round the block several times and this appealed to me.

His sartorial style was something that held less appeal. He really hated drawing attention to himself and in his efforts to look ordinary and fade into the background he dressed like a bank clerk from the 1950s, although his moustache was of the type favoured by film stars in the 1930s. He was extremely neat, even meticulous, about his appearance but he had no interest in fashion or fads. This was the era in which people were becoming aware of natural fibres but David's shirts were of drip-dry nylon. He washed them himself and hung them over the bath to dry. His overcoat, which dated from the 1950s, was a long, droopy gabardine of indeterminate colour and his ties were narrow strips of material from the same decade. He didn't see the point of buying clothes until those he already had were worn out.

– Four –

On those early dates David told me about his fear of death and his early boyhood dream of coming home to a house with a fire burning and a wife waiting for him. He also told me about an aborted romance with a girl to whom he had been engaged fifteen years earlier. He offered himself in these intimacies to a degree I could never match, although I don't think I knew this at the time.

On the whole, it was a relaxed and lovely time and I think that I, being a coward, would just have drifted on year after year, happy with the status quo. I knew that any idea of marriage would bring trouble down on our heads, so when David suggested it, I didn't say yes and I didn't say no but changed the subject, adroitly, as I thought. But he came back to it again and again and finally gave me an ultimatum. Either I agree to marry him or we would call it a day. I swallowed and smiled and thought of my Aunt Molly's happy, ten-year-long engagement.

I tried to think of delaying tactics but the best I could come up with was, 'Your family will be upset.' I knew this was nonsense. I had already met David's Dublin family – Louis and his wife Chookie and their boys – and they had welcomed me into their home with a warmth and sincerity I remember to this day. It was true that it would not be easy for his mother to accept me but she lived in London and David, who had been living on his own for more than a decade, was quite prepared to face any trouble that came along. I, on the other hand, was still living at home with my parents. Nowadays young people seem to get away as soon as they can but in those days in Dublin only country boys and girls lived in flats. The rest of us lived at home, the young women staying put, awaiting the arrival of Mr Right, who, as far as my parents were concerned, would certainly not come in the shape of a middle-aged Jew.

A child never grows up until he or she leaves home and I was far from being a grown-up. I was fearful of facing my parents but I was more fearful of losing David so one evening, after another pep talk from my beloved, I told my mother that I intended to marry the man who, as far as she knew, was merely someone who was helping me with my writing career, something she wasn't too keen on anyway. I had a good job as a teacher – why did I want to dabble in writing?

When I told her, she simply shook her head and said, 'You can't. He's not baptised.'

I knew what she meant: because David was not baptised he couldn't contract a sacrament; therefore we couldn't get married in a Catholic church. It never occurred to my mother that I would contemplate getting married outside the Church because, as far as she knew, I was still an observer. Actually, I had stopped believing in God somewhere in my mid-twenties but I kept this to myself and every Sunday I disappeared for a couple of hours, enough to keep everyone happy.

The logical place for us to get married – a lapsed Catholic and a lapsed Jew – was the Registry Office in Kildare Street, a dowdy, dusty place where the state, grudgingly, hosted such ceremonies. Mostly it was patronised by the marginalised – foreigners and divorced people, who, with due humility and gratitude, would keep their ceremonies low-key, with no long white dresses nor red carpets. I had already decided not to get married there because I felt I had caused my mother enough pain and the least I could do was marry in a church; the problem was, I hadn't thought about the obstacle of David's unbaptised status.

My brother, who is one of those annoying people who knows everything, came to my rescue. He informed my mother that we could get married in a church. 'A Catholic can contract the sacrament with a non-baptised person according to the Pauline Privilege,' he said.

Apparently this was something St Paul introduced into the teachings of the early Church when there weren't enough baptised people to go around.

My mother was annoyed by such laxity but she wasn't beaten yet.

'The Jews murdered Christ.'

'Christ was a Jew.'

Everyone knew this fact but certainly in the 1960s it was not consciously acknowledged by Catholics.

My mother had no answer to this.

I was speechless too but with relief. It was all out in the open now and it seemed that my mother had no more doctrinal objections to offer.

David, naturally, had assumed all along that we would have a civil marriage but when I explained why I felt I had to be married in a church he agreed to this, with one stipulation: he didn't want us to get married in Ireland because that would be rubbing his family's noses in it.

Where then?

Where else but in the heart of Catholicism, the Vatican itself? This was not as strange as it might seem and since those days it has become commonplace for Irish couples to get married in the Vatican State where a religious ceremony suffices as a valid marriage and there are no residency requirements. Along with these legal considerations, there is an embarrassment of churches to choose from, a great climate and great food in the many restaurants.

Having decided that we would get married abroad I thought it would be a good idea to throw a pre-nuptial party in Dublin.

We would invite our families and friends and I would invite my mother's friends too. I was an only daughter and I knew what I was depriving her of – a big wedding in my parish church, I in a white dress, she in a new hat. She would never be that mother of the bride so I had to offer a consolation prize.

We sent out the invitations, hired the Tailors' Hall, booked the caterers and bought cases and cases of champagne. If what we were doing was not quite kosher in the eyes of many, at least the entertainment would be lavish. I think we even had a string quartet playing in the minstrels' gallery.

I have photos of that party with my father raising a glass so he must have made a toast. David's brother and sister-in-law are looking lost and, although there is no photograph of my mother, I remember her, dressed in dark, funereal colours, clutching her handbag while her friends gathered round, offering support and sympathy: 'Sharper than a serpent's tooth…'

I remember too being approached by my Aunt Mary, who murmured as she gazed at David, 'Ah sure, he's a grand lad,' as if she had been expecting something else entirely.

Yet I enjoyed the night. All my friends were there, the venue was lovely, the wine flowed. I was marrying David and the hard part was behind us. Rome beckoned and two weeks' holidays with my soon-to-be husband.

Helen Lucy Burke was a great friend of David and when she heard we were getting married in the Vatican she said, 'Leave it to me. My sister, Priscilla, lives in Rome and she'll sort out all the details.'

Priscilla had a vision of how things ought to be done. She booked us into one of Rome's better and more expensive hotels, she chose St Anne's in the Vatican for the ceremony, found us an American Jesuit to marry us and decided that we would have our wedding lunch in a restaurant on the Via Appia just outside the city. All we had to do was turn up.

We left Dublin in the rain, augmented by my mother's tears.

My brother Conleth was coming with us: he was going to be one of our witnesses, the other being Priscilla. I had packed my wedding outfit, which, even considering the fashion vagaries of the day, now seems an eccentric choice. It consisted of a hand-crocheted lace blouse, an ankle-length báinín skirt and a long, hooded báinín cloak. I had bought the whole outfit in one of the small shops in Dawson Street that catered mainly for American tourists and I don't know whether I saw myself as some sort of Irish cailín or a walking advertisement for Bord Fáilte. One way or the other I was quite confident that I would be as bella a figura as ever tripped across the cobbles of St Peter's Square.

When all the practicalities were out of the way I began to feel sad. I knew how much I had disappointed my mother. My father had wished me well and returned to his books, something that made things worse. She would be on her own, mourning the loss of her only daughter, for whom she had had such high hopes. To her eyes, there was no way back from this disgrace. Marrying a Jew was somehow worse than living in sin or even having an illegitimate child. These things happened from time to time and although she was disapproving they were familiar transgressions. She knew nobody whose offspring had ever married a Jew. She thought I had ruined my life. I was a young woman with everything going for me and I was marrying a man twenty years older than me and a Jew to boot. I was furious with her attitude, which I saw as bigoted as well as disloyal – I was her daughter and she should have supported my choice rather than criticise it. I was, however, aware of the pain I was causing her.

My gloom lasted until we arrived in Rome; then that city took us under her wing and the three of us wandered around its streets, unsuitably dressed, for it had been a chilly late October in Dublin.

We were entranced.

Conleth and I considered ourselves old Italian hands for we had hitch-hiked to Florence a few years earlier and spent a week in a youth hostel there. Now we set about introducing David to the delights of Latin life. We drank too much coffee and too much wine that first night and ate far too much, explaining to David that all Italians ate pasta as a second course of a three-course meal and when in Rome…

Afterwards, we bought gelati and stood looking down into the brown waters of the Tiber. When we finally returned to our expensive hotel we retired to our separate bed chambers: I was getting married the next day and even if I wasn't leaving for the church from my father's house I was determined to observe as many conventions as possible, although I knew that we had both defied the convention that mattered to our respective tribes. It's lonely being different.

The next day, Priscilla took over. St Anne's, the church she had chosen, is one of those enormous, gloomy Renaissance buildings that abound in Rome. She hadn't thought of flowers but had hired a singer for the occasion, telling us that every wedding had to have music. The priest was a laid-back, American hippy who seemed to have woken up from a long sleep and he smiled at us encouragingly as we walked up to the altar. I don't remember being nervous and I had no reason to feel self-conscious for there was nobody else in the church, just the tiny wedding party of four and the priest and the singer.

The gloom, the empty, echoing church, the flickering candles, the hem of my báinín skirt rasping along the flagstones, the uncertain soprano suddenly bursting forth – I couldn't have invented such a wedding, a mixture of the Gothic and the bizarre. When I tell people about it they go 'Awww' in sympathy. But I was delighted with myself. I had got this far and David was holding up – it would be plain sailing from now on.

We exchanged our vows as David slipped a gold ring on my finger. Earlier I had suggested that he wear one also, but although there were many sacrifices he was willing to make for me, wearing a wedding ring wasn't one of them.

But the sacrifices he made were enormous and it was only

much later that I realised what it must have taken for him to get married in a Catholic church. Until I met David, anti-Semitism was not something I gave much thought to, seeing it more or less in connection with Germany and the Second World War, something that had existed in the past. Living with David I learned that it is more complex than this and that it lurks, like a virus, in hidden places and suddenly flashes into life. Of course, anti-Semitism has historically been fomented by other religions, especially by Catholicism, and the only example of formalised anti-Semitism in Ireland was the Limerick boycott of 1904, which stemmed from the preaching of a particular priest, a member of the Redemptorist order. So for David to marry me in a Catholic church must have taken a great effort.

Marrying out is more commonplace nowaday, as so many fewer people subscribe to any form of religion. Although David had no religious belief he had been brought up in what resembled a ghetto – a small, closed community that had little interaction with the outside world. In such a community, if anyone did marry out they were mourned as dead. Our marriage caused a rift in his family, with his two elder brothers disowning him. Nella, his sister, had no problem with it and she, Louis and his family were wonderfully supportive, as they have been ever since.

I wish now I hadn't taken David's sacrifice so lightly. For me, getting married in a Catholic church was a matter of convenience. I lacked the imagination to see things from his perspective.

None of this impinged on me as I crossed St Peter's Square, a married woman. A street photographer stopped us and when I look at one of the photos he took I see that David is very handsome in his wedding suit. It must also be said that I seem to be carrying off the báinín cloak with some élan.

Afterwards, on the Via Appia, we sat in the sunshine, a wedding party of five. It could have been a melancholy occasion with no members of either of our families present apart from Conleth but because it didn't resemble a wedding we could enjoy it as a party. Priscilla had ordered a Roman feast and we spent a long afternoon eating and drinking. There were no speeches, no good wishes from absent friends. I still have one of the little cups in which the wine was served. 'Hostaria l'Archeologia Roma' is written around its edges.

The next day Conleth went home and David and I began our honeymoon, a strange, ambivalent word with its undertones of waning moons and waning affections. For me it meant a holiday with a new spouse and new clothes. For David it also meant coping with the heat – even in October – and the food, both of which he did, stoically.

It wasn't real in the way that holidays often aren't. We lived on wine and sunshine with no thought of our lives at home and the problems that would face us, the first of which presented itself much sooner than we expected. When our holiday was over, as I left the unreality of Italy behind and climbed into an Aer Lingus plane, I heard the Irish voices around me and had a sudden realisation that the playacting was over.

We had gone to Rome and had had a great time but now we were returning to Ireland united in Holy Matrimony. I was a married woman and I didn't like the sound of that.

What had I done? Voluntarily I had entered into a prison, a cage, and, worse still, I was sharing it with a stranger.

The thought came from nowhere and with complete suddenness. I didn't know who this man I had just married was. I thought I did because we had spent time together, talked, exchanged ideas, disclosed weaknesses. But this was all surface stuff. Who was he? What was he really like?

I thought about my relationship with my blood family and saw that the myriad things I never had to explain to them because of our shared history – special family words, references, jokes – formed part of a language that David didn't speak. Why hadn't I noticed this before?

As the plane approached Ireland, I looked at the stranger

sitting beside me and my feeling of panic increased.

We drove in a taxi through gloomy streets to David's flat on Wellington Road. He had been living there for several years. I knew it well, I had spent nights there, but now I was seeing it through different eyes and this added to my sense of displacement and depression.

The flat was no more or less than your average furnished flat of the time, spartan and dreary. To be fair, it was probably no different from a lot of homes: this was before IKEA and Farrow and Ball and money and, again, to quote my mother, notions of style. However, although people in general had little awareness of individual style, most homes would have had some imprint of their occupiers. There was no imprint of David on this flat. There were no photographs, no pictures, no ornaments, no books left around. What sort of person could live like that?

In the bedroom his clothes took up about a fifth of the wardrobe space and one drawer of a three-drawer chest. They were all neatly stowed but cowering, as if apologising for their existence. The exception was a Noel Coward-style dressing gown, hanging on the back of the door. It was in a Paisley design and had a matching cravat and I never knew David to wear it except in hospital. It was the only cheerful note in the gloomy flat.

It was grey outside and chilly inside and I was too dispirited even to unpack my suitcase.

What have I done, I thought for the hundredth time as I brushed my teeth in dim light of the utilitarian bathroom? What have I done?

– Five –

In retrospect I think my reaction was quite normal. I had been so busy facing up to the forthcoming, unavoidable battle with my mother that I hadn't really thought about the marriage itself or what being married meant. I had jumped in, unthinking, as David's ultimatum won out over my mother's disapproval. Not until then did I really think about what I had done.

But next morning the gloom lifted and my feelings of the previous night seemed extravagant and silly. David might be a stranger but I had all the time in the world to get to know him. After he had left for work, I threw myself into my new role as housewife, knowing that this was all pretend as I had the luxury of a husband who saw me as a writer first and last and didn't expect me to spend my time cleaning and cooking. I felt lucky and happy but at the back of my mind I knew that I was avoiding the inevitable. My mother was living a few streets away and that I couldn't ignore this fact, unless I wanted complete estrangement.

The flat was small and eventually, having vacuumed and dusted, tidied and cleaned even the skirting boards and plumped up the cushions – something I had never done before in my life – I had to admit that there was nothing left to do.

I picked up the phone and rang my mother. 'It's me,' I said.

'Yes?' she said. Her voice was cold.

'I'm home.' Then I began to cry at the thought that I might have cut myself off from the only home I had known up until then, with her and my father and my brother.

My mother was a woman of narrow, unbending views and a fierce temper but she had a tender and forgiving heart. Like all of us she was a contradiction. Now she too began to cry.

'David's gone to work. Can I come and see you?'

'Come for your dinner.'

I was forgiven and within a few months David was accepted. Soon my mother was talking about what fine people there were in the Jewish community and after a year or two she took to ringing us up around Passover to ask us if we had seen the Chief Rabbi on the television and when we said we hadn't she would recount word for word what he had said.

But David never learned to relax in my mother's company – and who could blame him? He knew that he had had to prove himself to her, not because of any inherent shortcomings but because he was a Jew. He had lived through the war when all Jews went to bed with a suitcase packed in case Hitler invaded during the night. I don't remember that we ever encountered any overt anti-Semitism but I did notice that many people who were genuinely fond of him and delighted that we had got married, always, somehow, thought of him as not being Irish.

When they learned that he had translated Brian Merriman's *Cúirt an Mheán Oíche* into English they were genuinely astonished.

I was often asked where my new husband was from.

'Cork.'

'No, but you know what I mean – really from.'

'Cork.'

Meeting him for the first time people were often surprised by his Cork accent.

Jews were different; Jews were other, Jews were not really Irish.

None of this could really be described as anti-Semitism but it made David more aware of his otherness and, I think, contributed to his habit of solitariness. Coming back from our honeymoon I felt I had married a hermit. He had a few work colleagues and a friend in Derry and that was it. He hated going to parties and book launches and of course he didn't go to pubs, which was what really made him different.

In the 1970s in Dublin people didn't entertain at home and they didn't eat out in restaurants – they went to the pub. When we were going out together, David had offered me a different life – dinner in nice restaurants, visits to the theatre. It had seemed exotic to me then and I was happy to spend my evenings à deux. Now, however, I had just spent two weeks alone with David, I was embarking on married life and it was time to bring my husband and my friends together.

I suggested a visit to McDaid's, a pub frequented by writers and painters.

'You go if you like.'

'But I want you to come with me; I want you to meet my friends.'

'I'll be fine. You go off and enjoy yourself.'

It was David's very reasonableness that defeated me. He didn't mind my meeting my friends, he didn't object to spending nights on his own in the flat, he made no attempt to change me and was happy as long as I didn't try to change him.

I retreated in order to retrench but, ever-ambitious, thought I might take a stab at smartening him up. Years later I read a novel by Anita Brookner in which the young wife tries to transform her much older husband and I smiled in recognition.

I started by suggesting that he might like to wear sweaters at the weekend instead of the ubiquitous sports jacket.

'Why?'

'They'd be more comfortable.'

'The jacket is comfortable, there's nothing wrong with the jacket.'

'Would you think about a new overcoat?'

'What's wrong with the one I have?'

My next move was to buy him clothes as presents. He thanked me for them and admired them, then left them untouched in the wardrobe.

I nagged but soon found out that David was immune to nagging. Every time I came up against this stubborn streak I was surprised by it. Because our family always negotiated in the style of Violet Elizabeth Bott ('I'll thcream and thcream...') I kept on thinking that my smiling, softly-spoken husband would be a pushover. How wrong I was.

The one difference I did make to his wardrobe was to persuade him to get rid of the gabardine and buy a woollen coat, on the grounds that it would be warmer. It was a beautiful overcoat, navy with a red silk lining, and he wore it for the next twenty-five years, so that it went out of fashion and came back in before finally fraying beyond wearing. Nobody could accuse David of not getting value out of his clothes.

He never interfered with what I wore; in fact I don't think he really noticed. 'Very nice,' he would say as I twirled in front of him, all dressed up for some occasion. This was not very satisfactory so I stopped twirling. The one time he commented adversely on my appearance was when I had my long hair cut. Because he never seemed to notice how I looked I was surprised by how upset he was.

'You've ruined your beauty,' he said, with husbandly hyperbole.

'But all my friends say that it's much nicer and that it suits me.'

'They tell you what you want to hear,' he replied. 'But I tell you the truth.'

David was a romantic. He had fallen in love with a girl with long hair and as the years passed I remained the same girl. He never noticed that my jaw had begun to drop but he did notice when I cut my hair.

– Six –

One of my mother's gloomy prophecies was that by marrying an older man I would be marrying someone set in his ways. Much as I hated to admit it I could soon see that this was true. Some of David's foibles were hard to accept – the fact that he grew furious with me if I drank from 'his' mug, that I was not allowed to make our bed as he had his own way of making a bed, and that *his* chair was *his* chair. I found all this not only strange but insulting and unreasonable, especially the fact that I wasn't to drink from his mug: it was as if my lips on his lips were okay but my lips on his mug were *verboten*. He had lived on his own for so long that he found it upsetting if someone else – even his wife – touched his things.

I tried to talk to him about what I saw as absurd behaviour and, being angry, I'm sure I was aggressive in my approach. He simply closed down and I began to see that if we were going to live together, we would both have to change and make compromises.

I knew at this stage I was drinking too much, something highlighted by the fact that David was practically a teetotaller. With a little encouragement from him I was willing to reform but he would have to make an effort too, even if I were the one more in need of reform. When we had this discussion I discovered something about him that affected our lives together: David didn't believe that one could change. He was a fatalist and life was what it was.

This was so depressing a view that I decided to ignore it: I continued to try to change David and he continued to resist my efforts. Gradually I got used to him and to sharing my life with him. At some stage he stopped being a stranger, someone I had invented, and I began to get to know him as he really was. As I learned more about him, I learned more about myself. I had always considered myself an emotional person but now I saw that in comparison to my husband I was almost phlegmatic. This highly emotional temperament was why he couldn't risk having a row and it also explained his relationship with music. Music is the most abstract of the art forms, the hardest one to grasp if it doesn't immediately grip you around the throat as it did David. Music brought him solace and intensified his happiness. He spent hours listening to music, his eyes closed, unaware of anything else and in a state of bliss. I listen, I like, but I am not transported as he was. He told me that his first and true ambition was to be a concert pianist, something he could never hope to achieve as he had come to the piano too late.

For his eightieth birthday I bought tickets for a concert given by the great pianist Alfred Brendel. We settled into the back of the stalls and from the moment that the first key was depressed, David was beyond reach, in another world. At the interval or afterwards, he didn't speak. He didn't answer me on the way home – he didn't hear me. What he was feeling was beyond words, something he couldn't share. I don't think I have ever been so moved by a work of art or for such a sustained period and I envied him.

He was already suffering from dementia and gaining less and less pleasure from reading or theatre. But music, it seemed, was something he would continue to enjoy because it depended on an emotional rather than an intellectual response.

A great deal of music he dismissed. Pop music was just discordant noise, he loathed all forms of folk music and he didn't have any time for opera. Classical, instrumental music was what he loved and, following a long way after that, the great American singers and songwriters of the 1930s and 1940s.

I found it very unsatisfactory that he wouldn't have a decent row with me, hard as I tried to provoke him. I was used to rows in my own family: they blew up and deflated on a regular basis without any damage being done. It must have been because of this that I found the evenness of our daily lives a tad dull and on one occasion I kept goading him until eventually he gave me the row I wanted. The experience taught me a lesson: whereas afterwards I was happy to sit down to watch television, David could not. He retreated, deeply upset both by the things I had said to him and what he had said to me. He didn't sulk but he couldn't talk to me until the next day because the row had shaken him to such a degree. I was chastened and had sufficient sense to know that I would have to seek my excitement elsewhere.

I think, ultimately, that David's refusal to fight had a good effect on me as it made me less combative: I see an analogy between myself and Kate in *The Taming of the Shrew*. But although I do believe that marriage tamed me, I know that as a wife I was always a bit of a shrew. These are the sorts of regrets I have, remembering my sharp tongue that can wound without effort and that said things that cannot be unsaid.

David was mild and gentle by temperament and it was only in his relationship with the God in whose existence he didn't believe that he showed any hint of aggression. God was not a concept I spent much time thinking about, except sometimes to wonder whether he might, possibly, exist. I had assumed that David's attitude would be similar until I discovered how furious he could become with this non-existent deity. When some natural disaster like an earthquake or a tsunami occurred he would turn to me and say, almost triumphantly, 'You see what he's done now.'

'Who?'

'That – that – so-called God.' And he would point skywards. As he looked at the television screen at starving or injured people I could see him becoming angrier and angrier.

'But you don't believe in him,' I reminded him. 'He doesn't exist.'

'That's not the point – look at those poor people. Look at their suffering. How can anyone look at that and believe in a loving God?'

This is a question that has been asked through the ages but with David it seemed not an abstract question but a real accusation. It was as if he wanted God to exist so that there would be someone to blame for human suffering.

In his last years, when dementia had taken hold, he became even more preoccupied with God and when someone came to visit him or if he was meeting someone for the first time, he would look them squarely in the face and, without preamble, state, 'I'll tell you something now: there is no such thing as God.'

He wouldn't let it go – his disappointment wouldn't allow him to. Was it disappointment that God didn't exist or with the nature of a God who did exist? I was never quite sure.

Although David was an atheist he was also intensely Jewish. He was critical of Israel but believed that the Jews had to have a national home. He took great pride in Jewish achievement but also a certain delight in Jewish delinquency. If we were looking at the news on television and saw someone being arraigned for some swindle or other, he would point at the screen and laugh, 'One of the boys. At it again.'

'Ah come on. How can you tell he's a Jew?'

'I can tell. *Aithníonn ciaróg ciaróg eile.*' [One beetle recognises another.] And he'd laugh again.

– Seven –

In all sorts of daily routines David was very set in his ways and I never managed to change him. In fact, someone telling him what to do made him dig his heels in all the more firmly. However, in one particular and very important aspect he did change. When he married me he let his guard down and opened himself up to another human being. This was a profound change, a change that led to others.

He had been solitary all his life, from his teenage years when his best friend – a cousin – died. Later, he met a girl but when their relationship ended he resumed his solitary existence. During his thirteen years in London he made no friends and spent most of his time alone. There were one or two mates from work with whom he went to race meetings but no real friends. When he returned to Dublin it was the same story.

One could argue that this is a gender thing and that men, on the whole, don't have friends the way women do but David was not that sort of man. As well as being a feminist he was feminine in his emotional responses, something I recognised as I grew to know him better. His solitary life when we met was not one he had chosen but a result of disappointment and hurt having turned him into a virtual hermit.

Marriage changed all this. As he began to grow used to his new situation, to sharing and telling and listening, he began to invite other people into our lives, thereby chipping away at the carapace he had grown to exclude others and protect himself.

We became quite a sociable couple and David made new friends of his own whom he met independently from me. Sean McMahon, Vincent Banville, Tony Glavin and William Wall were men whose company he sought out and whose friendship he valued. He was not an easy man to befriend, although affable, for he was skilful at keeping people at arm's length. He was fearful of the Gentile world anyway, with its casual anti-Semitism, and he found male gatherings, the 'lads' en masse, distasteful.

These four men became his friends because they were so atypical: nobody could ever describe any of them as a 'lad'. For a start, they are all writers, intelligent and sensitive, and all very much aware of David's worth. He came to trust them and to relax in their company and in doing so he began to learn about the pleasures of friendship. He and Vincent had regular luncheon dates: it was luncheon rather than lunch, always in the Lord Edward, always just the two of them. They were quite similar in some respects: men of few words but with a ready humour. The others he met less regularly – Bill and Sean live outside Dublin and Tony had demanding family responsibilities – but he sought out their company and continued to see them even during his last illness.

When he was in St James's Hospital, dying, Tony came on his bike every week to visit him. David wasn't talking at all by this stage and didn't recognise anyone but Tony came and sat with him, faithfully, making time, however he managed it, in his busy life.

Sean brought gossip and a sharp northern humour. Erudite and a performer, he was very different from David, yet they had a bond and David always looked forward to his visits and took energy from them.

Through his friendship with Bill Wall, David rediscovered his native city. I love Cork, small and intimate, built on water, surrounded by gently rising hills, and it was wonderful to spend weekends there with Bill and his wife, Liz. The visits were so enjoyable not only because of the charm of their house, full of books and peace and warmth and a crazy dog called Trotsky, but because being in his native city somehow brought David alive, especially as he grew older. He took me to his old haunts, pointing to the scenes of past triumphs and disasters, all of them clear in his memory. On one occasion he even suggested that we move to Cork and I think if I had said yes we might have gone. But we both knew, really, that one can't go back and that these weekends were special treats. Our life was in Dublin and David would not recapture his youth by returning to Cork.

He has returned, now, his ashes scattered from the bridge over the Lee which he crossed on his way to school as a small boy. Some more of them are scattered in the Mardyke, where he lived, and in the park beside his house where he played cricket. Sarah and I, Bill and Liz scattered those ashes and it amazes me how important such rituals are and how comforting to those of us who are left behind.

David himself always claimed that he preferred the company of women. He felt less threatened by women and was more immediately at ease with them, another very singular aspect of his personality. Many Irishmen, even young Irishmen, are uneasy in women's company and prefer to spend time with the lads. With David this was reversed and because women could sense this they always responded to him. Val Mulkerns was a special friend, one of a very few from the old days, when as a young writer she and her husband-to-be, Maurice Kennedy, had contributed stories to *Irish Writing*. By happy coincidence we ended up living on neighbouring roads.

It was just as well I was not the jealous type for, throughout our married life, letters and phone calls came to David from women writers who had become good friends. As the years went by, the hermit I had married evolved into a sociable man. As he grew older, like all of us, he learned how to live better. For a man who had such a fear of death it was a strange and observable fact that in old age, as death approached, he grew happier. By then he had acquired good friends, a loving wife and an adoring daughter. He had armed himself against his greatest fear and learned to spend less time inside his head.

He went on making friends. Robert and Statia Bernen were living on a small farm in the Blue Stacks in Donegal when we got to know them. Bob was a classical scholar who had had an academic career in America before going to live in Greece and later in Ireland. I can understand why he went to Greece but I have no idea why he left it to move to Ireland. Neither of them had any connection with this country – he was a New York Jew, she a WASP from Connecticut. He was tall and understated and thoughtful; she was very handsome in a patrician sort of way and spoke like Katherine Hepburn. They lived in a cottage with no running water and their thirty-acre holding was a working farm, not something they played around with.

They must have had private means, however, because their clothes were expensive – not flashy, just expensive – and he was a member of one of the clubs on Stephen's Green. When they came to Dublin they stayed in the club and they would invite us to Sunday lunch.

The only other club I have ever been in is the Groucho in London, which was set up as an antidote to Bob's sort of club. But I loved the Dublin club. Entering there I felt I was entering into a world of make-believe. It was like having lunch with Lady Mary in Downton Abbey, no raised voices and old retainers moving quietly and only semi-visible, so discreet were they. The food was abundant, well cooked and unimaginative – just what one would expect.

Bob had written non-fiction before coming to Ireland; here he wrote his first short story and sent it in to New Irish Writing. Later on, Poolbeg Press published a collection of his stories called *Tales from the Blue Stacks*, a delightful book, now, unfortunately, out of print.

Our friendship with this interesting couple continued when

they returned to America. They would have remained in Ireland but Bob was diagnosed with multiple sclerosis and they both felt then that it was better for them to return to their homeland. When Bob died, several years ago, David mourned the loss of a writer as well as a friend. 'He was a real short story writer,' was the epitaph he gave Robert – the highest praise he could have offered.

Most of our friends were writers, people whom David had 'discovered'. I had many friends of my own but the majority of them never became 'our' friends, mainly because of David's diffidence in general company. With writers he felt more secure: to be fair, I think we both did. In the 1970s, Ireland was a very conformist place where you married into your own tribe, so our 'mixed marriage' made us different. The result among our civilised acquaintances was a determination to accept us utterly. They made a great effort not to offend in any way but this very effort made us uncomfortable.

Whether it was true or not, we both felt that writers and artists in general, being essentially outsiders, didn't have to make this effort because to them our marriage was no different from anybody else's. I think that at that time writers did lead less bourgeois lives: possibly because they were less accepted by society in general, certainly because they were poorer. Our non-writer friends didn't judge us but our writer friends didn't notice, so it was easier to spend time among the latter group.

– Eight –

If you had met David you would have found him self-effacing and modest, yet he had enormous reserves of self-belief. Here was a man who, as a callow youth, had persuaded established writers such as Edith Somerville to write for his magazine and now, in his fifties, an age at which many people are thinking of retiring, he embarked on a new career – he became a publisher.

He should have had enough on his plate already because by now not only was he editing New Irish Writing, he had become literary editor of the *Irish Press*. For many years Terence de Vere White had been cock of the walk over in D'Olier Street but David's page was soon giving *The Irish Times* books page a run for its money. He loved this work, choosing the books and matching reviewers to them. He was completely unorthodox in his choice of reviewers. Many unknowns were given a chance to shine, among them Con Houlihan, who turned out to be one of the best sports journalists Irish newspapers had ever seen. David didn't poach reviewers: he hunted for new ones. He would read an interview with a doctor or an airline pilot or an entrepreneur, find something interesting in the piece and file the name away for potential use as a reviewer. The *Irish Press* books pages covered a wide range of books and were not overly literary so they had a more general appeal than the usual books pages.

But David's chief interest still lay with the short story and it was concern for its wellbeing that got him involved in publishing.

Poolbeg Press was a joint venture between Philip MacDermott and David. Philip was a sales and marketing agent for several British publishers in those days and he and David used to meet in the Silver Swan pub, where David and other journalists went for morning coffee. New Irish Writing was publishing a short story every week and most weeks a new and talented writer was appearing. By the time their story was published the writers had usually embarked on a collection. The problem was: what to do with this collection? Then, as now, publishers were reluctant to publish collections of short stories – there was no money in them – so David decided that what was needed was a publishing house that concentrated on short story collections. As no such publishing house existed he would create one. By some means he persuaded Philip to join him in this quixotic scheme and Poolbeg Press was born.

I think they both put some money into the venture and, as I remember many closeted meetings in our sitting room between the two of them and Colm O'Briain, then chairman of the Arts Council, I imagine that the Arts Council also had an input.

Earlier in his life David had lost money on *Irish Writing* and now he was backing another outsider. I was not worried for, although David was a gambler, he was cautious and responsible and I knew he wouldn't do anything rash.

By the time Poolbeg Press had metamorphosed from a small, literary publishing house into a much larger and profitable purveyor of commercial as well as literary fiction David was long gone but he had a very happy ten years or so there, launching many grateful authors, including me, into the world.

It was a brave venture and quite cleverly thought out, somewhat along the lines of New Irish Writing. As well as publishing collections by new writers, David approached established writers with an offer to republish work that was out of print. Many of them were delighted with his offer. So a collection by John McGahern or Mary Lavin, for example, would be published side-by-side with some neophyte. This was a great fillip for the emerging writer and it gave status to the new publishing house.

Poolbeg Press was the precursor of many such small, literary publishing houses but it is hard for such ventures to succeed and well-nigh impossible if the publisher concentrates exclusively on short stories. In those early days there was a certain prejudice against fiction published in Ireland and it was harder to get it reviewed or noticed in the press. Then, when a writer became a success, he or she was immediately poached by one of the large publishing houses in England that could offer more money and the prospect of a wider audience.

Poolbeg lost a lot of ungrateful authors in this way, including me. In my defence I will say that I felt I had to find a publisher who wasn't my husband, even though David was my severest critic and domestic harmony was often disrupted when he didn't (or wouldn't, as I believed) see the inherent genius in something I had laid on his desk.

Losing authors, losing money, Poolbeg had to change: it did so by changing course towards more commercial publishing. Once this happened, David lost interest in the venture and withdrew, wishing it well.

Against all the odds Poolbeg, today, is more successful, bigger and more robust than anything David could have imagined. Of course, the face of Irish publishing has changed entirely. I have always thought, and still think, that without David as catalyst it might still be stuck in its old, narrow, dusty furrow, talented writers would remain unpublished and we would not have the numerous short story competitions that exist throughout the country to encourage new talent.

– Nine –

David was forty-eight when we got married, almost twenty years older than me. This was something that didn't worry either of us and never really impinged on our marriage. Having dated boys, I had found it a relief to go out with a man and David seemed unfazed by late marriage and later fatherhood.

However, as the years went on he did begin to worry at the prospect of my being left a widow. Although he never wanted to talk about dying or death, he sat me down one day and said with great solemnity, 'You must promise me that when I die you will get married again.'

This was not a conversation I wanted to have and I tried to laugh it off. 'Have you anyone in mind?'

'No, I mean it. You will be a young woman and I don't want you living the rest of your life on your own.'

My mother, too, worried that I would be left a young widow but, as it turned out, David and I were married for thirty-seven years, during the course of which I was to witness with sadness the much younger husbands of friends succumb to fatal illnesses.

I do sometimes think that what I missed out on by marrying an older man was the growing up together that couples experience when they marry in their twenties. David was confirmed in his way of life when I married him, the respective worlds of our youths were different worlds and there must have been distances between us of which I wasn't aware at the time. Although ours was a marriage of equals I know I deferred to him in many things. He didn't look for this but as he had seen so much more of the world than me and was less impetuous, it seemed his due.

Perhaps it was because of this that with marriage my life changed more than his: the biggest change was that I stopped going to pubs. In my single days most of my social life took place in McDaid's where I used to go with my brother Conleth or on my own because there were always people there whom I knew or half-knew. Often there would be a 'party' after the pub closed, which really just meant returning to someone's flat with six-packs. I saw the inside of a lot of grotty flats around Rathmines and the South Circular Road. There was never any food, unless we passed a chip shop en route, and very little snogging. We talked incessantly and drank and recommended books to one another and drank some more. It was a continuation of my student life and was easy and casual.

After an early attempt to get David to come to McDaid's with me I gave up and stopped too and became a wine drinker. I can't say I missed my old life as I was taken up with my new husband and now any spare time I had was devoted to trying to write.

David continued to listen to music and bet on horses. He kept up certain rituals, one of which was attending Royal Ascot every year. This meeting is held at the end of June and is considered the *crème de la crème* of the flat season. David had started going there as a child, when he was brought along by his father. Later, when he lived in London, he always went and now that he was settled back in Dublin and married he didn't see any reason why this should change.

I think I was more surprised than annoyed the first year to find myself deserted for more than a week by my new husband. He knew I couldn't go with him because of work commitments but he went anyway.

I found that I enjoyed that week of being on my own. I had no interest in horse racing and the novelty of having the house to myself, the sense of freedom it gave me, more than compensated for David's absence. I used to watch bits of the meeting on television, mainly to admire the fashion, which I wouldn't have seen if I had gone with David as he didn't go into the Royal Enclosure. It wasn't that he would have minded the cost of the entrance ticket but he would not, under any circumstances, don a top hat and tails. He hated what he called 'dressing up'. He was devoted to his sports jacket and on the occasions we got invitations that included the words 'Black Tie' he would say, 'That's me out, then.'

The only time I ever convinced him to wear a dinner jacket was for the opening of a Listowel Writers' Week. He was president at the time and the President of Ireland, Mary McAleese, was coming as guest of honour. The committee wanted him to wear a dinner jacket and I suggested that it would be a mark of respect for Mary McAleese for him to wear one. I went on at him until he agreed. He looked very handsome in it but how I regretted forcing him when I saw that the Martin McAleese, the President's husband, was wearing an ordinary lounge suit. David didn't even notice. Once the garment was on it was on and he forgot all about it.

During the Ascot meeting he used to stay in London and get the train to the course. Although he was staying with relatives, he never rang me during the week he was away: we were still in an era when international calls, nay, trunk calls, were reserved for announcements of birth or death. Nor did he bring me a present when he came home. This was another example of David's being his own man. He didn't understand the concept of exchanging gifts – they had never done it in his family, he said, and it seemed to him a senseless ritual. He felt the same way about Christmas or birthday cards, although he eventually had a Christmas card list of five people. One of the people on this list was Frank McGuinness, whose Christmas card was always the first to fall through our letterbox. It falls through mine to this day.

David broke the no-present rule on one occasion. He had had a particularly good Ascot and bought me a lovely coat. I still remember it – dark green, three-quarter length and with a belt. The size was perfect, as was the colour.

I would have thought that he had no idea about my size or what colour would suit me but I was wrong about this, as I was about so many things. I said I got to know David as the years passed but that is an exaggeration. He became a little less of a mystery to me as time went on, that's all. Now, thinking about it, I can see what prompted him to buy me that coat. He would not be dictated to by the convention of giving gifts on specific occasions, but after a good Ascot he was flush so it was natural that he would come home with a gift for me.

I did once go on a racing trip with him, one that he had cleverly disguised as a literary pilgrimage. One summer – maybe it was after a particularly good Ascot – he said to me, 'I know you're a great fan of the Brontë sisters.'

I agreed, wondering what was coming next.

'Then how about a trip to Haworth?'

We set out in my little Fiat and we did indeed visit Haworth and the parsonage and that haunting cemetery. But that was just the beginning of our trip. From Haworth we went to York and from York to Redcar.

'Great summer meetings,' David said. 'You'll enjoy them.'

It was a lovely summer that year and it was an enjoyable jaunt, driving from meeting to meeting and staying in nice hotels. Each day we followed a ritual. David was up early to buy the *Sporting Life*. After breakfast he spent the rest of the morning studying form while I wandered around the town. Then it was off to the races. I placed a bet the first day but was so outraged when I didn't win that I kept my money in my pocket after that. I am not a gambler but David would maintain that neither was he – that studying form and working things out were what interested him. He seldom made any money but he didn't lose much either for he was far too cautious to bet in large sums. He had no interest in jumps and little interest in Irish racing but devoted himself to the English flat season every year. Indeed, he might as well have been an observant Jew for all I saw of him on Saturdays, with the mornings devoted to studying form and the afternoons to looking at the races on the television. Sometimes now I turn on Channel Four on a Saturday afternoon and look at the racing for five or ten minutes and when I turn the set off I see him for a second sitting in his chair opposite, the *Sporting Life* open on his knee.

We don't really die when we die; there are still bits of us floating around until those who knew us and loved us also die and then, finally, we are gone.

– Ten –

David didn't really 'do' holidays; he was not good at being idle and liked to have his days organised and busy.

After that trip to Yorkshire we didn't go anywhere until Sarah, our daughter, was a toddler. When she was three or four we began to take her to the country or the seaside, where David would sit, fully clothed, on the sand while I played with her in the waves, except for one occasion when he donned his 1950s swimming trunks and joined us.

We were six years married before we became parents and this was mainly because of David's reluctance. In fact, if he had had his way we would not have brought a child into a world that for him was a place full of danger and pain. I knew that this was the way he felt and I didn't argue with him, partly because, even though I was in my early thirties, I was enjoying my life with David and was in no hurry to become a parent. We were really the first generation of couples who could plan our families because, by now, the contraceptive pill was available in Ireland. However, it was still not universally accepted and I remember the frowning disapproval with which my prescription was filled by a pharmacist in Rathmines.

Eventually, as friends became pregnant, I began to feel broody. I knew I would have to talk to David and sooner rather than later. Now that I had decided that I wanted to be a mother I realised that neither of us had time on our side. So one evening after dinner and a few glasses of wine I found my courage and told him that I thought it was about time we had a baby.

There was no confrontation: he didn't argue but he looked so stricken that he didn't need to. Eventually he said that he thought it was a bad idea, that he was too old, that the world was an awful place. We had many discussions along those lines and in the end he said that if I wanted to we should go ahead but...

I wanted to and I became pregnant and everything changed. David was as excited as I was and from the moment he saw Sarah's little bloody head peeping out of the white hospital blanket, he became his daughter's slave. Not that he was an indulgent father; he was much stricter than I was, especially when she became a teenager. This is a normal enough reaction and I think that an older father is probably more protective and more fearful. Not that David saw it like that: 'I know men' was his mantra as he tried in vain to keep his only child safe inside our Rathgar moat.

Once our baby daughter came home from hospital David was determined that, from now on, we would do everything as a family. For the first several years the only outings we had on our own were our Sunday afternoon visits to Sean and Eileen O'Faolain. For these we would leave Sarah with my mother, with David staring back at the house, not at all sure that we were doing the wise thing.

Sean and Eileen were good friends. When I visited them first with David, they lived in a house in Killiney with the most wonderful stepped garden overlooking the sea. Eileen was a talented, creative gardener and even when they moved to a much smaller house in Dún Laoghaire and she was no longer able to garden because of arthritis she directed operations from her sitting-room window.

Sean was a charming, sophisticated, interesting man. I always felt that he had never really got over his disappointment with the way the independent Ireland he had fought to establish had turned out. He was an intellectual and in Ireland we are suspicious of intellectuals. He had become one of David's regular reviewers and they were wonderful reviews: urbane, knowledgeable and witty. I think myself that he was more a man of letters than a writer of fiction, temperamentally more suited to the former.

When we started visiting, the O'Faolain Sunday gatherings could be quite glittering occasions with big-name writers and academics from the US and elsewhere. As time went on and Sean and Eileen got older – they were both the same age as the century – fewer people turned up and eventually it was often just the four of us. We were invited for afternoon tea until Eileen decided that producing this was too labour-intensive for them and from then on it would be drinks. This meant a sherry for David and a dry martini for me. They were of the generation for which drinks meant drinks before, as a nation, we all switched to wine.

I have happy memories of those Sunday afternoons: Eileen, frail and sitting propped up with cushions, could be quite wicked and was totally irreverent. Sean, who always had an eye for the ladies, would want to sit beside me but I devoted myself to Eileen because I found her less intimidating. I always felt with Sean that I had to perform and come up with witty ripostes.

But he was a joy to listen to, a wonderful conversationalist and not, like so many Irish people who undeservedly have this reputation, a monologuist. He asked one's opinion and listened to what one had to say. I always felt that he should have been living in a different country – France, perhaps, or a university town in New England, somewhere he would have found like-minded company. He also mixed a pretty potent dry martini.

When Eileen died, he was completely lost. They had been together since their student days in UCC. They had grown up together and grown old together and he never recovered from her loss. He developed dementia but, like David, his essence remained.

I remember taking him to lunch about a year before he died. It was a very surprising outing. I had thought that I would be more or less looking after him but once we got outside the house he became a changed person, as if part of him was remembering the man he used to be. He swept me into the restaurant, held my chair, summoned a waiter and when the waiter handed him a menu before handing one to me he pushed it away. 'Please – the lady first.'

He was a gallant, an old-style gallant. He was particularly fond of David, as Frank O'Connor had been. The Cork mafia was alive and well and always loyal.

We were a family now: David, I, Sarah and a cat, a cross-bred Siamese that David had named Vashti. He hadn't wanted a cat any more than he wanted a child ('We never had pets at home.') but I told David that a cat was the only answer to the mice that had recently taken up residence. My mother had a black cat with ideas above her station that mated regularly with the local Siamese lothario. It was one of their brood that we got and as David had become devoted to Sarah so he became devoted to the cat. She used to ride around on his shoulders and she was of great assistance to him when he wanted to make an early exit from a social gathering. 'We have to go home to feed the cat,' was a refrain that I became familiar with and, true to his word, the first thing he would do when we got home was to feed Vashti.

Sarah was born in March. I was on maternity leave which ran into the three-month-long school summer holidays so that our daughter would be almost six months old when I returned to my job. I knew how fortunate I was by comparison with other mothers and it never occurred to me that I would not return to work – I loved teaching and had wonderful colleagues and the school was just down the road.

One day I mentioned, casually, that I had an idea about someone who would mind Sarah.

'What do you mean?'

'In September, when I go back to work.'

David stared at me, his expression one of incomprehension. 'Go back to work? And leave our baby to be minded by a stranger?'

I began to explain that this woman would mind her in our house, that she was utterly reliable and a retired hospital nurse.

'She is a stranger. What if something happened to Sarah while she was being minded by a stranger?'

What if – such an unsettling little phrase. I began to imagine all sorts of unlikely happenings and by the end of the day I knew that I couldn't take the risk. My decision was illogical but irrevocable and naturally David was delighted.

'And you'll be able to write.'

I think he really believed this but of course I didn't write.

Nothing prepares you for motherhood, for the exhaustion and anxiety and the smug ones who look at your howling baby, pat you on the back and say, no, they never really had any problems with their darlings. Maybe you were a bit tense?

Sarah howled: for the first five months she howled for hours and drove me to distraction. I was breastfeeding her with gritted-teeth determination and she was putting on weight so I reckoned that she wasn't hungry. She didn't have a dirty nappy and she was sleeping soundly in between the bouts of howling. What on earth was the matter with her?

I took her to a paediatrician who looked at me over his half-moon glasses, smiled his condescension and shrugged his shoulders. Nothing wrong; just pay my large fee on the way out.

Now I really began to resent David. Sarah did most of her howling during the day and by the time he came home she would be either asleep or lying peacefully in her basket. At weekends, to give him his due, he took her out in her pram, which gave me a chance to hang out line upon line of terry-towelling nappies that seemed to take weeks to dry. He wasn't at all anxious about his daughter, which surprised me, and he was willing to help but, as he could neither feed her nor cook for me, he wasn't of much practical use. None of this bothered me: what made me resent him was the ease with which he fell back into a deep sleep each time we were woken up during the night. Sarah would cry and I would wake him up and he would go and get her from her room next door. Then I would begin to feed her and before I had finished, David would have returned to the arms of Morpheus.

When the feed was over and the baby returned to her own room I would flounce back to bed, thump my pillows and turn and twist while my husband slept on, undisturbed.

I bought a bottle and a packet of formula and prepared it for the first night feed. I would still get up to heat the bottle to the proper temperature but I believed that in time I could entrust all this to David. He would do a night feed and even if I was awake too I would have the satisfaction of knowing that he was sharing the task.

But Sarah, even at this tender age her father's daughter, refused to cooperate. She would not take the bottle. It wasn't the formula she objected to but the teat. I tried again the next day but she simply refused to have that teat in her mouth and I was back to square one.

I was to feel a similar resentment eighteen or so years later when Sarah was out at one in the morning, having promised faithfully to be home by twelve. I never slept while she was out and as twelve o'clock became a quarter past I would get up, put on my dressing gown and stand at the front door, waiting for the taxi to draw up.

David, meanwhile, would snore on. When I shook him awake he would open one eye, mutter, 'Don't worry, she'll be home soon,' and turn over, asleep again within minutes.

It was only when we became parents that I realised that David, unlike me, didn't suffer from anxiety. Perhaps it had something to do with his fatalism but he never worried, as I did, about what might happen. Was this just our individual natures or had it something to do with our upbringings?

'Please, God, don't let it happen,' I still find myself praying in moments of distress.' Jews don't pray for help, only forgiveness.

I grew more anxious when I became a parent, expecting

something awful to befall my baby if she was out of my sight, whereas David only began to worry at a later stage, not an irrational anxiety, as he would see it, but because 'He knew men'.

So we became a traditional family – Daddy going out to work every day and Mammy staying at home to mind the baby. Except that by 1980 this was no longer the norm in Ireland. Most women who had jobs that were at all well paid went back to work when their maternity leave was over and, besides, there were very few young mothers living in our area.

I sometimes wondered if there were suburban estates with lots of young mothers supporting one another, while I spent my time pushing my pram around the streets, just to get out of an empty house and hear voices other than baby gurgling. Those big old prams with the giant wheels made things difficult, for they were cumbersome and took up too much room to be parked in a coffee shop. So I had my coffee at home, alone and looking out at a neglected garden. I couldn't really read as I was sure to be interrupted. The one thing that saved my sanity was the radio. I became an obsessive radio listener and among our daughter's first words were, 'Order, order,' which open the Radio 4 programme, *Yesterday in Parliament*.

My friends were mostly working and those with small children lived too far away for a casual visit. Our road was a mixture of flats and houses, many of the houses occupied by elderly people who had lived there all their lives. This had been ideal in my childless days when I had sneered at suburbia and all that it entailed. Now I longed for companionship, for other mothers who, instead of discussing the Booker shortlist, would talk to me about nappy rash and weaning.

Another aspect of full-time motherhood was the shock of suddenly not having any money of my own. I had always worked and even as a schoolgirl I had my savings from summer jobs. Now, if I wanted to buy anything I had to put my hand out to David – or this is how it appeared to me.

We had always had separate bank accounts but at this point David suggested that we have a joint account, a suggestion I vetoed. I agreed to a housekeeping kitty – I didn't feel guilty about this and I had to eat. Then David said that he would put so much per month into my account and I could spend it whatever way I liked. This was reasonable, he said. I was working as a full-time mother and housewife so why should I not be paid?

I found it practically impossible to touch that money and, for the most part, bought any personal stuff with the interest from a small savings account I had.

I had no job or money and I was lonely. What many regard as a period of joy was difficult for me and in my eyes it was all David's fault. I now realise how neurotic my attitude was but being isolated with a small baby was not something I found easy. As Sarah grew older things got better. I grew more used to her and saw that she was designed for survival even if I didn't hang over the pram or cot every moment of the day. I began to enjoy my new life and, as David had predicted, I eventually began to write again. Looking back now I think he was right and that I wouldn't have produced any more work if I had gone back to teach. In the great scheme of things that wouldn't have mattered much – it's about choices and we can travel down only one road. But I am glad now that he uttered those words, 'What if?' and that as a result I stayed at home with our daughter.

When I look at Sarah's contemporaries, many of whose mothers went back to work after maternity leave, I can't honestly see that having a stay-at-home mother has benefited my daughter especially. The gain was mine, for once her babyhood was over I really began to enjoy my life at home with my toddler. As she became a little person with a distinct personality we began to have fun. Children are so interesting if one has time to observe them – to notice how they change, how their minds are growing every second, absorbing everything that comes to their attention. Beyond a certain point it all becomes tedious but there is tedium in every job and I know that I led a privileged existence with only one child to mind and enough money to allow me not to worry.

I see the stressed faces of mothers as they drop their babies off at the crèche round the corner from me and I know that being a working mother of small children is not easy.

– Eleven –

Because of the huge success of New Irish Writing David had
acquired a public profile and couldn't remain entirely hidden with
his wife and daughter in Rathgar, much as he would have liked
to do so. When Sarah was nine, he was invited to give a series of
talks across America, not so much as a writer and editor but as that
extraordinary phenomenon – an Irish Jew. After all, as a young
man he had written a short story named 'Who Ever Heard of an
Irish Jew?'

He felt he should go on the tour but he agreed only on
condition that his wife and daughter could come along too, so
we set out for the US, *terra incognita* for all of us. We arrived in
Boston, where he had his first engagement. We stayed in the
homes of Irish-Americans, extraordinarily generous and trusting
people who opened their houses to us and sometimes left us
there on our own if they had engagements elsewhere. We went
from Boston to Pittsburgh, where it was snowing and a bear
was roaming the suburbs, with warnings on the radio. From the
snows of Pittsburgh we flew to San Antonio in Texas where we
stood in our woollens watching a parade of Mexican-Americans
in temperatures of 21°. Then it was back across the continent to
Albany, the capital of New York State, a small, conservative city
that reminded me of Ireland in the 1950s. At this point we split
up, Sarah and I travelling to New York City while David went on
to the Twin Cities of St Paul and Minneapolis. When Americans

we met heard that we were going to New York they warned me to be careful and watch my pocketbook. There were so many tales and warnings and I was so terrified that, when we arrived at Grand Central Station, I was afraid to make eye contact with a kind man who held a door open for us.

We stayed in Lower Manhattan with an Irishwoman who had a loft apartment – the first time I had heard that expression. That night she took us out to look at the Twin Towers. They were just around the corner from the apartment and a must-see for tourists to that part of the island.

Angela Carter, our hostess, owned the Keshcarrigan Book-shop. Like me, she was a Leitrim woman – Keshcarrigan is in County Leitrim – and, like me, she had a Jewish husband. She was a very busy woman and the next morning she took us to the subway and left us, patting me on the shoulder and telling me that it was safe and simple to use. Eventually we found the train that would take us to the Upper West Side where we were to meet a friend for lunch. As we settled in, surrounded by black youths with giant trainers on their large feet, someone lobbed a brick through our window and we were all ushered on to another train. Already those warnings I had heard from provincial Americans were coming true.

We met our friend in the restaurant of the Metropolitan Museum. He was a New Yorker and the first thing he suggested was that I join him in a dry martini – shaken, not stirred, of course. This was more like it. I forgot about the brick and from then on began to enjoy New York, a friendly, relaxed city, not unlike Dublin, just on a bigger scale and with those sky-scrapers enclosing the sky. In fact, although much of America seemed very foreign to me, New York felt familiar, like another European city, despite the architecture.

The next day David arrived, full of talk about his experiences in the Twin Cities. I could see how much he was enjoying himself – he seemed like a different man. He was full of energy and enthusiasm and although he was by then in his early sixties he seemed to thrive on his tough schedule. As the trip continued, he hopped from city to city, got on and off trains and planes and gave readings and interviews. For someone who normally shunned the limelight he really enjoyed this new life. He had flirted with the possibility of emigrating to the US when he was a young man and might well have done so if the war hadn't intervened. Now I watched him, easy and relaxed in this wide-open society, and wondered how different his life would have been if he had gone.

Europe killed off most of her Jews but in America they have thrived. From my little knowledge of that continent it seems to me that an American is an American before he is a Jew or Gentile and I saw David become a participant rather than an observer as Jewish-Americans and Irish-Americans gathered round and questioned him and marvelled at him. Nobody paid any attention to the fact that he had a non-Jewish wife – marrying out had been going on for a long time over there.

Sarah too had a great time; she was at a perfect age for such a trip, old enough to be confident but before the self-consciousness of adolescence had descended. In Barnes and Noble she went up to the desk and explained to an assistant that both her parents were writers, asking if they would see to it that their books were displayed on the shelves.

When the servers in restaurants filled her glass with ice, she said no thank you, explaining that we didn't have ice in Ireland so she didn't really want any. 'Cute kid' was the usual comment. Sarah would give a gap-toothed smile and we would look on proudly. Children are admired in America, encouraged both to be seen and heard.

Before this trip I had never had any desire to visit the US and I think this was because I was snooty and superior about Americans, considering them naïve and unsophisticated. I believe now that anyone who visits the country comes away with a completely different impression. America is a continent and Americans come in every shape and type: the most sophisticated, the most intellectual, the most naïve, the stupidest. What unites them is their amazing friendliness and the hospitality and openness they show their visitors. The positive attitude that is everywhere to be seen is refreshing for jaded and cynical Europeans. We have no reason at all to feel superior.

– Twelve –

Our trip to America unsettled me and I began to yearn for further journeys abroad. I had been an eager traveller as a young woman and now I thought that we could start taking holidays somewhere in Europe, as Sarah was of an age to enjoy them.

Of course, I knew perfectly well that in general David hated Abroad, which began for him at Dún Laoghaire pier and anywhere north of the Gate Theatre, but, still having learned nothing, I was sure I could change all that. Now I had Sarah as an ally so it would be two against one. I decided that we would go to the south of Spain. I had spent time in Spain as a student but I had never been to Andalusia. I chose Nerja on the Costa del Sol because I had heard somewhere that it was a quiet, sedate resort far, far from the madding crowds of Torremolinos.

It was a wrong-headed decision for me to make, knowing as I did that David could not tolerate hot weather – if the temperature went above 18° on a summer's day in Ireland he would complain. I think part of the reason we ended up in Spain was that I felt he had no right to complain about the heat because, unlike me, he had skin that tanned in minutes. By the end of our normal summer he would have acquired a farmer's tan with brown hands and neck showing beyond the edges of the sports jacket. What right had someone as lucky as that to complain about the sun?

So I dragged him off to Nerja to a jerry-built apartment without air conditioning. The traditional houses in this part of

Spain have thick walls and small windows, built to withstand the heat, whereas the newly-built apartments had paper-thin walls and large, plate-glass windows. There is nothing to do in such places except sunbathe and swim, which is precisely why people choose to go there. By late morning the temperature would have risen to the high 20s, sometimes 30°, and the sky would remain that merciless, metallic blue, so different from what Irish people are used to. I spent the day at the pool down below playing with Sarah while David languished, shirtless, up on the third floor. For that whole week he was like Count Dracula and ventured forth only after dark. Then he would don a shirt and the three of us would wander along the seafront before finding a restaurant in which to eat dinner.

It wasn't my sort of holiday any more than it was David's and I should have known that most of the Costa del Sol had been blighted years before by mass tourism. There seemed to be few Spaniards around and the other visitors were mainly older English people. In this respect I had been right: Nerja it wasn't as raucous as the other resorts along that coast. It was so sedate as to be boring.

In making my choice I also had Sarah in mind. She was entering her teens and I wanted her to fit in. She had enough to contend with already – an only child, a much older father and parents who both felt themselves to be outsiders. The least I could do was to offer her the sort of holiday that so many of her friends were having.

We endured that boring holiday and David never complained. He didn't complain anyway. If he really didn't want to do something, he didn't do it; otherwise he put up with minor inconveniences in silence. He never once said 'I told you so,' as we passed by restaurants offering roast beef Sunday lunches and ye olde English pubs selling Guinness – thankfully, it was before the advent of the Irish pub abroad. David had a great capacity for putting up with things, something that was not entirely healthy for him. He also wanted to make us happy.

– Thirteen –

In this book I am trying to give a sense of David – the sort of man he was. He liked to plan everything and led an ordered life, his routine predictable and unchanging. Then, out of nowhere, he would come up with a suggestion that surprised all of us, even him.

For example, a year or two after our trip to Nerja he came home from work one day and said, without preamble, 'How would you like a trip to China?' This was not long after the 1989 student protests in Tiananmen Square that had been so brutally put down by the authorities.

I don't remember what I replied – I was probably too surprised to say anything.

'We're going there. I've booked our tickets. We're leaving from London. And remember, this is it as far as I'm concerned – no more foreign travel.'

'But – where did the idea come from?'

'I got a bargain.'

China was trying to rebuild its tourist industry and David could never resist a bargain – or so I thought at the time. Now I feel there must have been something more than this to prompt him to make this decision. At this time, very few people were travelling to China, twenty-two hours' flight from Dublin, an unknown world where we wouldn't even be able to read the street signs. To suggest a trip to such a place suggests a real spirit of adventure, something I had never seen in David. After nineteen years of marriage I still didn't know him.

We joined a group of about twenty other people, mainly English, in London, and set out for Beijing, travelling with Air China. It was a daytime flight with a stop in Sharjah in the United Arab Emirates. The most exciting thing was flying over the Himalayas and seeing their snowy peaks reaching out of the clouds.

In Beijing we stayed on the seventeenth floor of a skyscraper hotel; thankfully, the lifts were efficient, although always crowded. The first thing I noticed about the Chinese was how adroitly and gracefully they moved, navigating crowds with great skill. All our activities were organised and we toured the vast city and took trips to visit the Great Wall and other tourist sites. It was on the first of these bus trips that David again surprised me. As we sat in the bus, waiting for our driver, a young woman from Belfast stood up and announced that money would have to be collected to tip the local guides on each outing. Nodding towards David she added, 'Our barrister from Dublin has agreed to take on this responsibility.'

I looked at our barrister from Dublin and wondered, firstly, if he had introduced himself thus and, secondly, if he had volunteered for the task? Had the idea come from him? In fact, how on earth had he and the young Belfast woman started a conversation? My shy, retiring husband was full of surprises.

The one independent outing we had during the holiday was to a silk market where I persuaded David to buy himself a pair of silk pyjamas. They were grey-and-white-striped and became his favourite sleeping apparel, so comfortable, so cool. Sarah and I bought embroidered dressing gowns – I still have mine.

I don't know how interested David really was in China and the trip was a bit of an endurance test. The weather was hot and we were constantly travelling or sightseeing, on top of which he was struck down on more than one occasion with Beijing belly. This was hardly surprising, for the food was a challenge for all of us. We could have 'European', which consisted mainly of bacon and egg, or Chinese, delicious on the whole but sometimes off-putting when you looked at your plate and saw an eye staring back at you.

I imagine that there were many occasions as we wandered around in the dusty heat that David wished he had resisted that bargain.

What I remember most vividly is not the delights of the Forbidden City but the hundreds of cyclists six or seven abreast on the streets. I remember too one occasion when we were coming down in a funicular railway and Chinese tourists in an ascending car began to take photos of us – strange, round-eyed, white-skinned devils.

David was true to his resolve and after our trip to China there were no more foreign adventures for him. He was not a good traveller. The heat upset him, he hated hotels, foreign food upset his digestive system and he felt threatened and uneasy outside his own environment.

By this time we had begun to take fewer holidays as a family. Sarah was reaching the age when she was spending summers in Europe to improve her proficiency in the languages she was studying and without her we stopped taking holidays in Ireland. David had no interest in the great outdoors or beautiful scenery, being a city man at heart. I, an adopted Dubliner, never really understood how someone who came from Cork could be described as a city person – apologies to all Corkonians (some of whom are my best friends) for such crassness. But David was essentially urban; he liked the encirclement of city streets and the anonymity of crowds. Paradoxically, he felt safer in a city.

– Fourteen –

Of course the outstanding event in our married life and the thing that most changed our lives was the birth of our daughter. Of course becoming a parent changes everyone but I am surprised, looking back, to realise that David was more changed than me by this huge happening. I was busier, doing the nappies and the breastfeeding, but David was undergoing an enormous psychological metamorphosis. I was exhausted; David was a different man.

He remained fearful, maybe more fearful than ever, but now he had to let hope in. This scrap of mewling humanity was flesh of his flesh and whereas religion or even love didn't offer a bulwark against death, the birth of his daughter did.

What was particularly lovely was how much his daughter Sarah turned out to be. When she was little I saw her more as mine – after all, we were the same gender and I had given birth to her. But she was having none of it. Being an only child and with an innate sense of fairness she always treated us with meticulous evenhandedness and as she grew older I had to acknowledge how many traits she shared with her father. Temperamentally they were very alike, emotional but gentle, whereas I am less emotional and a bit of a scrapper. They were both reflective by nature and more naturally solitary than I am. They shared that profound response to music which I don't really understand. No doubt about it, she was his daughter as much as she is mine.

We sent her to piano lessons when she was about seven – I think she had expressed an interest in playing. She progressed from a local teacher to the College of Music, where Miss Markie took her on. After a couple of years, although Miss Markie judged that she 'had a nice touch', David declared that he would no longer pay for lessons because Sarah was not practising. I tried to convince him that it was a question of keeping her at it until she got to the stage where she began to enjoy playing but he was adamant and the lessons were abandoned.

He had come to the piano as a teenager and had always felt that this late start meant he could never really catch up. Now his child was being given a brilliant opportunity and couldn't be bothered to spend half an hour every day practising. He was so disappointed in her that he wouldn't try to coerce or even persuade her – she should have seen, she should have known.

I think that this is an example of David's emotional nature and his stubbornness leading him to a wrong decision. When Sarah was older she regretted having given up the piano and when she was studying in St Petersburg she found herself a teacher and took it up again.

Throughout David's life I saw examples of what might be regarded as unbending harshness but, which were, in reality, always a reaction to his disappointment in someone. He was disappointed in Sarah, so no more lessons.

The same thing happened with a journalist whose writing talent he had discovered. This man, now dead, had become prominent in his field, largely due to the initial help David had given him and, while they weren't really friends, there was warmth between them. But he borrowed money – some small sum – from David and never repaid it. He was that sort of person – careless, charming and easygoing. David never asked for the money back; he simply cut the man out of his life.

It was a harsh reaction but he had liked the man and he was disappointed in him. Because I often behave badly I have a tolerance of other people's low standards – but not David.

Apart from the débâcle of the piano lessons, he was never disappointed in Sarah. She went to work in London and at an early stage in his dementia she asked him to come and spend a weekend with her, just the two of them. When I went to pick him up in Dublin airport on his return I found him wandering around, disorientated. This was obviously a manifestation of the disease but it was also that he had just come back from Lyonnesse and he couldn't see properly because the magic was still in his eyes.

It must have been a wonderful experience for them both. He was returning to a city where he had spent many lonely years, sharing it now with his newly grown-up daughter, showing her places he had worked as she showed him her new life. They went to a concert in the Royal Festival Hall, which had played such a significant role in his London life and which continued to be a presence in our lives in Dublin: from time to time he would say to me, 'I've booked tickets for the Festival Hall.' For him our National Concert Hall remained for ever the Festival Hall.

David and Sarah exchanged weekly letters and their closeness and mutual love were a great consolation to David as he grew older. Physically she is very much a Marcus and I can't see any of my genes in her; yet nowadays, when I look at her little son, I see my mother staring back at me and I realise again that people don't die when they die.

– Fifteen –

It took me a while to realise that I was married to a silent man: possibly not until Sarah had left home and the two of us were on our own. While she lived with us there was always something to talk about – mainly her – but after that I seem to remember us sitting in silence, particularly at mealtimes. David was not a natural conversationalist: he never speculated, never took delight in allowing the talk to loop around, to repeat, go back, correct, imagine. All this he found tedious. 'Chatter', was the term he used to dismiss it and, although he was normally the least sexist of men, he deemed it a female vice, as well as a national one. Female and Irish, I was doubly condemned.

A silent person is never a problem in company as most people are only too happy to fill in the gaps, especially in Ireland; living with one is different. I was determined that I would make a talker out of David and spent many evenings trying to get a conversation going. I never succeeded and as the years went by I too became silent when we were together. I never noticed the change until, towards the end of his life, when he was developing dementia, he became almost loquacious and I found myself answering in monosyllables. I wasn't trying to get my own back after all the years of silence; I had simply lost the habit of conversation with him.

Nowadays as I sit on a bus and listen to the conversations going on round me, I notice how often people repeat what they say two, sometimes three times, changing a word here and there but essentially saying the same thing. I think of David and smile: he was right about this as about so many things. Chatter – a national vice.

But when I am feeling more self-critical I think that I might have driven him into silence for surely in the early days after we met he talked with ease? If I hadn't talked so much *at* him, he might have been encouraged to say more. He had a friend whom he saw less and less of because she talked so much. 'That incessant voice goes through my head,' he remarked once and now I imagine that I might have had the same effect, chattering away at him, driving him more into himself. Or I may have frightened him into silence. I am very opinionated, as were all my family: in our house there were constant discussions – mainly about politics – during which opposing views were shouted down without rancour and with much enthusiasm.

I think this style of discourse intimidated David.

You're wrong.

Just nonsense.

Absolute rubbish.

Such bald statements in the course of an argument never seemed unreasonable to me, much less rude. David, being milder, less opinionated and with better manners, probably saw them differently: he retreated into silence, which, of course, gave him the moral high ground and left me feeling defeated.

A silent person is unsettling and I was often left wondering what he was thinking, what was going on inside his head. Did he see me as a harridan? Had I been shouting? I still don't have the answers but I am left with a sense of my own raucousness and loudness. I remember the sharpness of my tongue, the ease with which I would use any underhand method to win an argument. I regret this very much and wish that I had been more aware of his quieter personality that maybe needed encouragement to talk.

I am not suggesting that David was an easy person to live with. *Au contraire*. In theory he was a perfect husband. He didn't drink, didn't smoke, rarely lost his temper, made no demands and never tried to impose his will on me. I thought for a long time that this attitude was admirable but as time went by and we began to spend more time on our own I began to feel that it was a sort of fatalistic indifference that caused him to accept me as I was. David was detached from life, which meant that he was also detached from marriage. It is hard to explain what I mean by this because we loved each other and I know that I made him happy – or as happy as he was capable of being. One of the first things David told me about himself was that he had a terror of death. He was laying his cards on the table when he said this, warning me, but I didn't see this and treated what he told me lightly. It seemed to me a reasonable fear. After all death for most of us is the elephant that never leaves the room.

Because of David's temperament his fear wasn't apparent on a day-to-day basis. He was not a gloomy person; he was even-tempered and seemed contented. He didn't sigh in corners, he was never visited by the Black Dog that haunted Winston Churchill; he seemed far happier than many people I knew. So I didn't give much thought to what he had told me and when I did it seemed to me that he was dealing well with his anxiety. I saw his fear of death as that – a phobia, an anxiety, a neurosis that he managed to control. He smiled, he enjoyed life, there was nothing for me to worry about and anyway we all suffer from such existential worries.

In fact, David's worries were of a different order. I now believe that he really did live in the shadow of death, that every waking moment he was haunted by it and that as a result he lacked a commitment to life. This meant that he was incapable of experiencing the sort of joy we feel when we wake up on a lovely, sunny morning and think that it is good to be alive.

I can and do get depressed, I have moments when I cannot see the point of our existence but I have many more moments of delight – random moments, when the sun warms my face or I watch a child in a pram or have my first sip of wine of an evening.

Then I know that the world is good, no ifs or buts.

This is the state of healthy denial in which most of us live. We ignore the reality of death because the pull of life is stronger. With David, the current was running in the opposite direction. He could not really commit to life because he was so aware that it would be snatched away from him one day. He didn't worry about me being knocked down by a bus or Sarah dying of some infant disease. We were all going to die and his obsessive awareness of this truth made the time and means almost irrelevant.

Most people are not paralysed by this awareness: we get on with things, we invent eternal life to see us through the night. This David could not do but I think now that if he had had help he might have learned to do so. I should have listened more carefully the first time he disclosed his fear to me. We were newly married at the time, a period when disclosures are made and both partners are at their most malleable. I might have done something to help him but I dismissed what was an intimate admission, believing a fear of death to be a logical response to our human dilemma. How could there be psychological help for it?

Nor would it have been easy to sell him the idea of any kind of psychological help – I can hear him now denouncing such things as mumbo jumbo, declaring that there was nothing wrong with him, or nothing that could be cured by a lot of charlatans. But I could have tried.

Marriage helped him a bit, being a father helped a lot but ultimately the fear of death never left his consciousness. Living with this was not easy for him; nor was it easy for me and it did affect our marriage.

Now that he is dead and I can't change his sadness or my in-adequacies I try to remember that our life together was not gloomy and that for most of the time we were happy. Even though David was anti-social by nature he seemed to enjoy the dinner parties we gave. We were in our own home and would have chosen the guests so David was relaxed. He was an attentive host, offering aperitifs and pouring the wine and telling stories about his days as the young editor of *Irish Writing*. I had discovered that I liked cooking so I enjoyed myself too.

What David didn't enjoy were casual encounters and in this respect his job was a help to him. Editors are often shadowy characters whose names and work we know without having any idea of what they are like or even look like and this was what David wanted. He did meet young writers as he had met me, bringing them in to talk about their work, but these were one-to-one encounters with a specific agenda, a non-threatening situation. Otherwise he guarded his privacy and rarely went to book launches or other literary events. Although he corresponded for years with many of Ireland's leading writers he seldom met them face to face.

All of this was to change with the establishment, in 1971, of the Hennessy Literary Awards, in the course of which he found himself entertaining not only Irish writers but foreign luminaries. These ceremonies were a far cry from our safe little dinner parties and he brought the whole thing on his own head.

David always felt the short story was a form unjustly overlooked in favour of the novel. It was because of this belief that he instigated the annual Hennessy Awards. Sponsored by the eponymous drinks company, they were given yearly to people whose original work had appeared during the course of the year in New Irish Writing. All work was eligible, there was no shortlist and there were two judges – one Irish, one non-Irish. The non-Irish judge was essential, David believed, to keep nepotism at bay.

Every year the judges and winners assembled at a reception hosted by Hennessy in a beautiful house in Mountjoy Square where the company had its headquarters. The presentation of awards of any kind can be a yawningly boring occasion – even, sometimes, for the recipients – but this was never true of the Hennessy receptions, which I remember as occasions of fun and hilarity and sometimes misrule. I think that this was due to a combination of the quantity of Hennessy brandy that flowed and the high spirits of the visiting judges, released from their garrets for the night.

I remember one occasion when a beautiful young PR woman burst into the reception, looking hot and slightly dishevelled, closely pursued by the non-Irish judge, who had a distinctly lascivious gleam in his eye. This writer was then enjoying a high profile after the huge success of his new novel and the PR woman had collected him from the airport in a taxi: unfortunately, she was far too discreet to tell us what might have happened on the journey into town.

On another occasion, when the Irish judge discovered that the winners of the awards weren't being invited to the dinner afterwards, he spent fifteen minutes insulting his hosts – from whom he had just received a handsome cheque. Then, in case the French ambassador, who was the guest of honour, hadn't understood his tirade, he translated it into perfect French.

The visiting judges often spent an extra day in Dublin and when they did we would have them to dinner in our house. One man, a writer from the north of England, banged the table and denounced what he called our elitism when he discovered that our names weren't listed in the phone book.

'What's so special about you? Do you think you are better than a plumber or a miner? You won't find them making themselves ex-directory.' He spoke the last words with a sneering distaste.

We had taken our names out of the directory on advice from the Gardaí after a bomb scare incident the previous year but the writer wasn't to know this and neither of us could get a word in edgeways to enlighten him.

V.S. Pritchett was the nicest judge we ever had to dinner and William Saroyan the most emotional, weeping into his beef stroganoff as he recounted the fate of the Armenians. 'We suffered genocide too, the Jews are not unique,' he said, looking balefully at David.

David and he became good friends and corresponded regularly after that meeting and after William had signed for him a battered copy of *The Daring Young Man on the Flying Trapeze*, the 1934 collection that had kindled David's love of the short story.

Maeve Brennan was a writer we both admired and I was excited at the prospect of her coming to dinner. We had arranged to collect her at her hotel but when we arrived, she had checked out, leaving us no message. Maybe it was just as well because at that same meal, another of our writer guests quickly polished off whatever he was eating and then calmly reached out his fork and began to help himself to his neighbour's food.

David presided over these occasions with benign good humour. Although in general intolerant of bad behaviour, he granted his guests a certain licence because they were writers. But this did not extend to a particular midnight caller who arrived at our gate after the road had settled down to sleep. 'Come out, David Marcus,' he howled. 'Come out and explain to me why you wouldn't publish my story. Come out you b......d and face me like a man.'

David was far from being an action man but he hopped out of bed, put his gabardine on over his pyjamas and went outside to confront the wounded writer. 'A child asleep inside...' I heard him say as the writer began to apologise. 'Get home now – you should be ashamed of yourself.'

David also invited some of his reviewers to dinner. Someone I particularly remember was the novelist Patrick O'Brian. He later became famous in Ireland and England because of an exposé in the *Sunday Times* that claimed not only that he not one of the O'Briens of Inchiquin but that he was not even Irish.

When we met him he lived in the south of France, away from the literary world, known only to a select group of readers, fans of his cultish series of novels about the Royal Navy during the Napoleonic Wars. I've tried without success to read these books but I know that others are devoted to his work.

If he was a chancer he was a very charming one. He did claim to be Irish and while he didn't actually say he was of noble lineage he told us that his family had originated in County Clare. When I asked if he was related to Lord Inchiquin he didn't demur but smiled modestly.

I can't remember what we ate but I do remember the wine. This was the time when Irish people were beginning to drink wine with their meals, something almost unheard-of until then. Although I knew nothing about wine I had the confidence of the ignorant and it never occurred to me to ask for advice. Instead I went off to the local supermarket and bought a litre bottle of Hirondelle which I proudly sat on the table.

I am sure some of my readers will remember this mass-produced French wine, which was at that time the plonk *du jour*. Manfully, Patrick took a sip, then, turning to me with a smile, he said, 'You are quite right. When I serve a small red I never bring it up to room temperature either.'

Someone to whom I told this story felt that he had insulted me but I think he handled the situation gracefully. For anyone with a palate – and Patrick had his own vineyard – it was probably undrinkable stuff, whatever temperature it was served at. He couldn't honestly say that it was a good wine but he made a comment that made me feel like a connoisseur. To this day I continue to drink 'small' reds cold and with total enjoyment.

Of course the whole incident went right over David's head. By this stage he had started drinking a half-glass with his Saturday dinner but wine was wine and he knew what he liked. What else was there to be said on the subject?

As for Patrick O'Brian, I think that he was just a harmless snob. He was also delightful company and a great raconteur. I have always retained an affection for him, even after the *Sunday Times* revealed his feet of clay.

– Sixteen –

Since David's death, and especially since beginning to write this book, I have spent much time reflecting on his life. During the course of our thirty-seven-year-long marriage I learned how high David's reputation was in the work he did. I knew this but I never thought about it, never stopped along the way to ponder what a talented man my husband was.

Now looking back I do believe that, among many other things, he was that rare phenomenon – a great literary editor. He had studied law at university and his lack of a degree in English always made him believe that he was not a critic. And he wasn't, insofar as he didn't speak the language. Literary criticism is often arcane and precious and can be intimidating to the uninitiated. For that reason David would never talk books with literary coves but this didn't really matter: he had that essential requirement for a good critic – an unerring nose. Because he was an outsider he was never influenced by literary fashion; in fact, he wasn't even aware of what it was. This kept his olfactory sense pure and allowed him, right into old age, to recognise talent.

I observed this one year when I was a judge in a short story competition. Once we judges had made our selections and passed them on, the people who ran the competition allowed David to see all the entrants. This happened with a number of competitions because, although he was no longer editor of New Irish Writing, he edited an annual anthology of Irish short stories for Faber so he was still on the hunt for talent. On this occasion, David read through all the entries, put some aside, then chose one. It was not our winner, nor our second choice, although it did get a prize. I think we were right not to place the story any higher – it had flaws and was not as successfully realised as the more highly-ranked stories – but it was this story that drew his attention.

All the entrants were anonymous and it was only at the prizegiving that David got to meet the writer whose story he had chosen. She turned out to be Claire Keegan, who became a good friend to both of us. Claire is, without a doubt, a major talent. But the fascinating thing for me is that David could see this already, when she was still at the apprentice stage, just embarking on her writing career. I believe that one can improve greatly as a writer and that most writers do improve through learning their craft and practising it but I also believe that there is such a thing as an inherent talent which sets a very few writers apart. This talent can neither be learned nor improved on and it was such a talent that David saw in Claire's story.

How did he do it? How did he see that inherent special quality in the midst of more accomplished stories offered by writers of lesser talent?

A nose for literature, just as rare as a nose for wine – that's what David had. William Maxwell of the *New Yorker* had this gift, as had Frank O'Connor. O'Connor spoke and wrote about the 'voice', which is the instrument of the writer as much as it is of the singer and which is the reason one writer thrills us and another interests us mildly.

Great editors instantly recognise the voice, even at the stage where it is struggling to emerge. Claire Keegan's was the last voice David recognised in his long career as an editor. He was dedicated and hard-working and he never lost his enthusiasm; even as an old man he would get excited when he discovered a new writer. These were the qualities, together with that nose, that made him a great editor.

– Seventeen –

I might have been less surprised by some of David's major decisions had I remembered that I had married a gambler. Although he never spent much money on the horses, in other aspects of his life he took huge gambles. He grew bored easily and with boredom would come a desire for change. Before Sarah was born we were a two-income family and reasonably well off. When David persuaded me to become a full-time mother he assured me that, as our mortgage was almost cleared and he was earning a decent salary, we would be fine. And indeed we were, although I continued to worry about money.

As time went by, his salary increased and I began to relax. We didn't live extravagantly and seemed to be doing all right. Then one day, out of the blue it seemed to me, he came home and announced that he was giving up his job at the *Irish Press* because there was a novel he wanted to write. By now he had severed the connection with Poolbeg but he was getting a state pension and he assured me with great confidence that he had worked the whole thing out. We owned our own house; he had savings; there would be no problem. Except for our growing child who like most middle-class western children must be supported by her parents, at least until her early twenties.

I had sleepless nights but David was adamant. I tried to persuade him that he would grow bored. He loved his work and meeting his reviewers and the young writers whose stories and poetry he published. I knew by then how isolated a writer's life could be and what if there were two of us, tap-tapping away in separate rooms with not a single fresh idea wafting in from the outside?

I also knew that whatever I said I would not be able to change his mind. He left the *Irish Press* because he had grown bored with it, just as earlier on he had grown bored with his editing life in Cork and later with his insurance job in London. Many of us grow bored with our jobs but feel we have to stick them out. David, being a gambler, took a chance.

In his early life, he had written poems, translated *The Midnight Court* from Irish and completed a novel, *To Next Year in Jerusalem*, which was published to great acclaim, all while he was still in his twenties. The novel was also published in America. It sold better than most first novels and was widely reviewed in Ireland and in the UK, so the beginning of his career as a writer was more auspicious than most. However, his next book was rejected, so he turned away from writing, deciding that he didn't have enough talent. It was quite extraordinary that he should return to it in his sixties but in character with the way he had lived his life, taking chances.

His second flowering produced two novels – *A Land Not Theirs* and *A Land in Flames* – a collection of short stories – *Who Ever Heard of an Irish Jew?* – an autobiography – *Oughtobiography* – and a fictionalised autobiography, *Hidden Memories*. He was particularly pleased with the title of the autobiography, as punning was one of his weaknesses, as well as being a family weakness. When he and Louis met there was always lots of punning and laughter and mutual appreciation.

Many writers do a bit of editing and many editors are writers manqué but neither of these situations applied to David. He was a legendary editor and a very successful writer but he wasn't confident as a writer and dismissed what he produced merely as 'tales'. I don't agree with him in this assessment of himself but I think that he was not enough of an egotist to take his own creative work seriously. To be a writer you must believe in yourself, in your importance and worth and value, but in this respect I could never persuade David to take himself seriously. This may be why he never gave the same attention to his own work as he did to the work of the writers he published. He was impatient with what he produced, rushing things out, wanting to get the book published as soon as possible, whereas his advice to his writers would always be to go back and see if they could improve on what they had written.

He thought of himself as a teller of tales rather than a serious writer and his novels could indeed be described as 'tales'. Serious writing demands a lot of introspection, searching through detritus which it might be safer to leave undisturbed. David was a secretive person and, while we are all secretive to a degree, I think David kept secrets from himself. We are back with the emotional man, the man who was afraid to look too deeply into his heart because if he did he might be undone. I think David sought an antidote to this fear by telling tales rather than writing stories but the tales he told were engaging and he told them well. His books were popular and sold well and he enjoyed his late success, happy to go anywhere he was asked – to signings and bookshops and book festivals. His fans came out in their legions. He had been good to many aspiring writers and they in turn were happy to see him published and to support him.

He began to receive the public recognition I always felt was his due. Kenny's Bookshop in Galway held an evening in his honour, attended by friends and writers from all over the west of Ireland. His native city and his alma mater, University College, Cork, both recognised him: he became a freeman of Cork and an honorary doctor of his university.

He still had energy and enthusiasm and there seemed every reason for him to go on writing but again he surprised me and changed course one final time, having heard the siren call once more. There was talent out there waiting to be discovered. It was at this stage that he approached Faber with his last big idea.

By now, the *Irish Press* had closed but New Irish Writing was appearing in the *Sunday Tribune* under the editorship of Ciarán Carty. David felt that there was room for another enterprise. His idea was to edit a yearly book of Irish short stories for Faber, chosen exclusively by him. He knew he still had his nose and it had begun to itch.

This is another example of his self-confidence as an editor. He was at an age when most people have retired, he had no infrastructure – no office, no secretary – yet he approached the leading literary publishing house in Britain, sure that they would run with the idea. They did. So he set up a post office box for himself to which manuscripts would be sent, got in touch with many of the writers whom he had discovered and put an advertisement in the literary pages of the newspapers announcing his new venture.

Of course the project was a success and the stories came pouring in. Twice a week he would walk down to Rathmines with an empty shopping bag and bring it back full of manuscripts. The process was the same as it had ever been. He would read every story that came in to him, consider each one, choose those that he could see promise in, write to the authors and arrange to meet them in the café of one of the bookshops in town, an appropriate choice and with no alcohol to lead aspiring writers astray.

For David, choosing a story was a very personal thing and it was important for him to meet the author. Normally he shied away from meeting new people but writers were different: he felt safe in their company, a confidence that was naïve but also romantic. Many of our greatest writers have held unsavoury views but David was in love with the whole business of writing and writers for him were on a different moral plane from everyone else. He accepted worse behaviour from them than he did from other people, although, on the whole, the writers he mentored were on their best behaviour while in his company. His formality set the tone but with that formality went warmth; there was nothing stiff about him.

I had not been keen on this venture and tried to persuade him against it, fearing that, as the elderly man he now was, he would meet disappointment. In this situation I was pessimistic but David, although a total pessimist with regard to the big questions, was always an optimist in everyday life. The anthologies were a success and seeking talented short story writers kept him busy and happy until his illness began to impair his judgement and his energy began to flag.

– Eighteen –

Living our lives we don't stop to analyse them and retrospective analysis runs the risk of being both dishonest and inaccurate but I have attempted to understand the man I married and the life we shared for almost forty years. David remains a mystery to me, yet I know aspects of him, shards that were revealed over the course of a lifetime. He was fearful and brave, sad and merry, silent, self-effacing and self-confident, introspective and kind. Above all, he accepted the world as it was and didn't try to change it. For me this was difficult.

But that's less than half the story and the other half, which I have had in my head for years, I now find I have to edit and change in an effort to make it more honest and less self-serving. I always saw myself as the open person in the marriage – ready to bare my soul, to share, to give of myself – whereas the husband I invented was closed, secretive and silent. There is some truth in this picture. I laughed and joked or shouted and stamped my foot and told David that I was happy or sad or angry. But this was all fairly superficial stuff. There were things I never shared with him – weaknesses, shame, desire – things that remained hidden, that I couldn't admit to.

Over the years, David did withdraw but if I look honestly at the time when we were first married what I see is a husband who was more willing to open up to me than I was to him. He was willing to let me in because, for him, this is what being married meant. From those early days I remember conversations in which he revealed himself and let me see parts of his heart.

And me? I think I was more ambivalent. This is something I realise with surprise even now, for the vision I have of myself as frank and open persists. I *am* those things – but only to a certain degree. The things about myself that really shamed me I couldn't tell David – I couldn't even tell myself. I pushed them away into such a deep recess that they were virtually irretrievable. The result is that what I feel today is a mixture of guilt and shame. This may partly be due to my Catholic upbringing: I know that David felt neither guilt nor shame the way I did.

I wasn't good at being married in those early days: not only was I unable to share my secrets, I didn't want to hear his. I wanted to keep at least a part of me intact and standing alone. I was incapable of holding his hand, closing my eyes and jumping into the unknown along with him.

Marriage is such a strange and interesting institution. I remember when I was a girl worrying whether I would be able to put on my make-up in the morning before my husband woke and saw my naked face. But the intimacies of marriage are all-embracing. In sickness and in health means sharing at close quarters all those embarrassing little illnesses like diarrhoea or piles or even a nasty cold when your nose runs with snot and your eyes are red.

Your toenails grow too long and you scrape your partner's shin or you drink too much and have to retire to bed with a bucket. Over the years, if the marriage lasts, you stop thinking of your secrets as secrets; eventually, unconsciously, you let your guard down, you get used to the other person being in your life and forget to hide yourself away. You become half of a couple. And we did, despite me and my shame.

For David and me, physical intimacy was never a problem, which it was for lots of couples in those distant, guilt-ridden days. This helped our marriage over hurdles, helped it to solidify and evolve and last. We were faithful to each other. David was, by temperament, uxorious whereas I might well have had a fling. I understand why people are unfaithful and believe that infidelity often isn't of all that much significance to the erring partner, no more than a minor transgression. I'm inclined to agree with this view; it's what comes afterwards that is problematic. David would have felt betrayed if I had strayed so if I had, it would have necessitated deceit. I believe that there is no room for deceit in a marriage; it is dishonourable and deliberate in a way that infidelity may not be. David and I had different moral values but the outcome was the same – a faithful marriage for both of us.

My marriage was also a refuge for me, somewhere I knew I would find support and comfort. Throughout the years we were together David was strong and steadfast and loyal – above all, loyal.

An incident that occurred when David was in his mid-seventies demonstrated this clearly to me. I was driving us over to the Writers' Museum on Parnell Square one wet, dark, November evening. As we crossed O'Connell Bridge, I felt something bump against my car. I saw people stopping and a Garda making straight for me. I had knocked down a cyclist.

I was sober and in plenty of time for the event but I was angry about something and maybe arguing with David and not paying enough attention to the road. I wasn't aware that I had swerved and I never saw the cyclist until after I had felt the bump.

It was a nightmare, its awfulness mitigated only by the fact that the poor man I had knocked down was not seriously hurt – just a grazed hand, as I remember. The Garda took details from me and I suppose from other witnesses and a week later David and I were both summoned to our local Garda station where we were interviewed separately.

At the end of the interview the Garda suggested that David, being a barrister, had been coaching me but this was completely untrue. David had been consoling me, telling me to state exactly what had happened as he intended to do but pointing out that it was important for us not to compare notes. Above all, he reassured me that I wouldn't go to jail, for at this point I saw a stretch in Mountjoy looming.

He never criticised me, never suggested that I could have paid more attention to the road. He supported me and I could feel his non-judgemental presence throughout the whole ordeal – calm, solid and loyal.

I felt awful, guilty and worried about the man – not a young man – whom I had hit while he was cycling home from work. The case was sent to the DPP and I was told that I could be charged with dangerous driving (in fact I wasn't). I kept thinking of the man, who got older and more decrepit and poorer in my imagination every day and I decided to send him a cheque to try to make up for the trauma I had caused. Whatever way you looked at it – whether he had swerved into my path or I into his – I was the one in charge of the lethal machine and therefore responsible. Luckily David saved me from myself, pointing out that by sending money to the man I could be seen as trying to bribe him.

When I think back over this incident I often wonder if I would have behaved with such loyalty if the situation had been reversed. Would I have supported David without a word of criticism the way he did me? I hope so but sometimes I think I wouldn't. He had moral qualities that I know I lack.

– Nineteen –

As Sarah grew up, going through school and on to university, David remained a relaxed parent, apart from his constant awareness of the danger of the lurking male. His daughter was a paragon but he knew men. Luckily for all of us, Sarah showed more interest in ballet than boys during her teenage years and by the time she started in Trinity David had begun to think that perhaps his daughter also knew men.

When she was twenty-three she told us that she intended to leave home. We had been very close as a family, doing a lot together, spending time with one another because we liked one another's company. But David and I agreed with her that she needed to move away, away from our endless, overwhelming interest in everything she did. She was the centre of our world but it would be very unhealthy for all of us if we were to become the centre of hers.

So we encouraged her out of the nest, even as our hearts ached. We both thought that this would probably mean a flat at the end of Rathmines Road but Sarah, being her father's daughter, did nothing by halves. At this time there were jobs to be had in Dublin but she wanted something more: to spread her wings and see a bit of the world. When she told us she was off to London we accepted her decision meekly, like generations of parents before us.

We both knew how much we would miss her but I imagined that it would be worse for David, who was older now, his world already shrinking. Again I underestimated him. There now began an epistolary relationship between father and daughter that suited them both. It kept them close and helped to assuage loneliness, which Sarah was also experiencing as a newcomer to a vast metropolis. Their weekly letters crossed the Irish Sea without fail. I never read either side of the correspondence as I felt it was something special between the two of them. I had my phone calls and, later, text messages; they had their weekly letters.

As David got older and dementia began to take hold, he began to boast about his only child. In the end, it seemed as if she were running a publishing empire. But although he got the scale wrong, what he was basically proud of was the fact that our child, brought up by hand, was forging a life for herself in a foreign city – with some success. It is harder for an only child to cut the apron strings because he or she has more responsibility and to walk away seems a much more significant act. Sarah did it and I think that while we were proud of her for doing so we were also proud of ourselves for letting her go without complaint. Now I see her with her small children and wish that David had lived long enough to see them too.

To my surprise I found that I missed Sarah more than David did. He was as busy as ever with his Faber anthologies whereas I found that a great expanse of emptiness had opened up in my life. I was idle, bored and purposeless so I decided that I would get back to some proper, disciplined writing.

Somewhere during Sarah's childhood I had abandoned my schedule of writing every day and as a result I had produced little. Now I thought that if I returned to my old working habits I would begin to produce work on a significant scale again. So I sat down at my laptop and thought and tinkered but after about a month of this I gave up. I had nothing to say; I was finished, washed up. I became angry, both with myself and with David, blaming him, irrationally and unjustly, both for Sarah's departure and for my ever having embarked upon a writing career. If I hadn't listened to him I would have a job now, money coming in, an interesting life. It was all his fault, leading me on, encouraging me to think of myself as a writer. If I had been depressed I might have done nothing but my anger urged me to action and suddenly, almost unaware of what I was doing, I began to change my life. Always someone with little interest in physical activity. I now took up yoga, joined a gym for a while and became a serious walker.

Such activities held no interest for David. Why would they? Approaching eighty, he had not even a twinge of arthritis so he didn't need yoga to keep him supple. Going for walks he found pointless and a bore, although as he did not drive a car he did walk.

In other aspects our lives were changing too: we were entertaining much less because the whole business of giving dinner parties seemed suddenly too much without David's help. He had never cooked but he had poured the wine and looked after the guests but now these tasks began to agitate him. If I had been alert I might have paid more attention to what I believe in hindsight to have been an early manifestation of the onset of dementia but I just thought of it as David getting older. Gradually our social life together began to tail off.

We grew apart – or rather I grew away from David. I spent less time at home. I didn't want to be at home because now that I wasn't writing there was little for me to do. This might not have mattered at an earlier stage in our marriage, as we had always led fairly independent lives. But now David was old and needed special kindness and care, while I was out and about, angry with everything and trying to prove I don't know what. Not that there was anything pathetic about him. Physically he wasn't all that changed from the man I had married and it wasn't as if he were idle when he was home by himself. He wasn't neglected, we still spent almost every evening together and what I think I feel guilty about is the fact that I didn't want to spend time with him. Being married to an editor and a discoverer of new talent had always been something I was proud of but now it just reminded me of my own failure. Better to go off to my yoga classes and concentrate on my breathing.

This turning away from my dear husband is something I bitterly regret and that I can never put right. I didn't know it but there was little time left for us together. The only consolation I have is that I honestly think David hardly noticed. The yearly anthologies were throwing up lots of new writers, as David knew they would. His eightieth birthday was approaching and he was as purposeful and busy as he had ever been so I never really worried about his health. There was no way I could have been forewarned.

One morning he went off to see one of his writers and about two hours later I had a phone call from her warning me that there was something wrong with David.

'What do you mean – what's wrong with him?'

'I don't know but you'll see. He's on his way home to you now.'

He managed to find his way home, which surprised me when I saw him because he was talking gibberish. When we saw our doctor he told me to take him to a hospital emergency department. There we sat from five in the afternoon until one in the morning before being seen by a doctor. By this time he seemed to have improved but he was admitted to the hospital. Later in the day when I came back to see him he could talk intelligibly but he couldn't read a newspaper or write a sentence.

The diagnosis was that a blood vessel in his head had burst and he had had a bleed into the brain. Apparently this is a random event that can happen to any of us at any time and can cause anything from minor and temporary impairment to death, depending on the size of the bleed.

David's bleed was small and after a week in hospital he was discharged, on no medication and back to his old self, as we both thought. Because he was so healthy in general, neither of us was worried. He had two older brothers who were thriving and his family was long-lived.

Life went back to normal and David was soon working as hard

as ever. Up before me every morning, he had finished his breakfast before I came down. He always made his own breakfast – a slice of white toast and a cup of coffee with two spoons of sugar. After we got married I had tried, without success, to get him to eat brown bread. Although he was not a practising Jew he still adhered to certain dietary rules. He didn't eat pig or shellfish and although I have always loved bacon I never cooked it in our house. I used to buy certain Jewish foodstuffs that he liked – wurst, a kosher sausage that is cooked in an omelette; chopped herring, another delicacy to which he was partial. You could say we were a semi-kosher household.

I understood why he would not eat pig – he had never done so and it would be like my eating dog. Once we were invited to dinner at a house in which, ironically, the host was a Jew. The centrepiece of the main course was a splendid baked and glazed ham. I thought David would simply refuse it but he didn't and on the way home I had to stop the car and let him out to vomit on the side of the road. He had suffered because he hadn't wanted to embarrass his hosts. Sometimes he carried good manners and consideration too far. But he really had no interest in food and was happy as long as he could indulge his sweet tooth. When he was returning from the bookie's office he often dropped into the supermarket to buy a packet of biscuits, just in case I had failed to bake a cake or make a pudding.

Then, shortly after coming out of hospital he decided that he needed a bit more variety in his life and said that he wanted to start cooking. Although he had lived by himself for sixteen years he had never cooked anything except what he called a pancake: a sturdy and rubbery dish containing a huge quantity of flour and an egg. Apart from that, when I met him first he was living on tinned fish and tinned vegetables, lots of white bread and lots of biscuits.

Now when he expressed an interest in taking up cooking I was surprised but delighted. I had many Jewish cookery books and I got them down and suggested that he should look through them to see where he would like to start. He already knew: he wanted to start (and, as it turned out, finish) with bananas. He liked bananas and was sure there must be plenty of ways of cooking them. And there are – banana fritters, banana pie, baked bananas, glazed bananas – he tried them all. For a while we ate a great many bananas and he became such an adept cook that he didn't need my assistance any longer and would shoo me away, then with a flourish produce the finished dish. However, when I suggested that he move on to something other than bananas, he lost interest and that was the end of his cooking career.

We both soon forgot about David's burst blood vessel for he continued in remarkably good health. He was on no medication of any kind right up to his death and when he was past his mid-seventies he took great pride in the fact that he could still run for a bus. Every night he slept, undisturbed, for about seven hours.

All his life he had taken his good health for granted and with the exception of those sprints to catch the bus he took no exercise and ate what he liked. What he liked were refined carbohydrates and a lot of sugar. Amazingly, even his teeth were good. He never put on weight and it was only towards the end of his life that he developed that old-age skinniness. Maybe the athleticism of his youth stood to him. He had played table tennis for Munster and also played football and cycled distances of up to thirty miles. When he was in his seventies he discovered a veterans' table tennis club around the corner from us and decided he'd have a game. He went in with all paddles blazing and nearly killed himself. He had to be assisted home and he was too exhausted even to undress. He was pale and shivering and he frightened both of us.

Next morning I asked him what on earth he had thought he was doing.

'I thought I was young,' he said.

– Twenty –

Human beings are adaptable and I began to get used to Sarah's
absence. I noticed that she was settling into her new life in
London. She emailed or phoned, telling us about new friends she
had made, things she was doing and places she was visiting. She
was beginning to enjoy life in a big city.

This made her absence more bearable and me more contented.
I found that I was no longer angry and although I continued with
my new pursuits I didn't feel there was a distance between David
and me. Our life was beginning to return to what it had been in
the early days. I never worried about the fact that David was now
an old man. Despite his age, in many ways David hardly seemed
changed. He had lost his hair in middle age, so no change there.
He remained pink-cheeked and wrinkle-free and continued his
daily walks to and from Rathmines, boasting to me, when he came
home, of the number of walkers he had overtaken on his way.

But we live our lives in a constant state of flux and just as I
thought we had reached some sort of plateau, I began to notice
certain changes in David's behaviour. They were small things,
easily overlooked, and I did ignore them for as long as I could.

As we get older, most of us begin to forget things, then start
worrying that it is the beginning of Alzheimer's. But David's
memory was always better than mine. It was something else that I
was picking up: increasingly, he didn't seem to understand what I
was saying, even when I said it a second time.

For example, I'd tell him I had cooked salmon for our dinner and he'd reply that he hadn't bought any salmon that day. This was harking back to his bachelor days when tinned salmon was one of the staples in his diet. Or if I suggested that he take his umbrella as it was looking like rain he'd reply that there was no need for me to buy an umbrella as he already had one.

At first I tried to convince myself that all this was nothing, that David's hearing was causing problems or that he hadn't been listening to something I said. Eventually, however, I had to admit it – David was having difficulty in processing what was said to him. I was frightened and this led me to deny what was happening, in the hope, I suppose, that it would disappear. It didn't get any worse but it didn't go away. He got a hearing aid but it made no difference and I began to discuss my worries, telling his family and one or two close friends what I feared. Dementia is hard to spot in the early stages and everyone told me that David was fine and that I was worrying unnecessarily. He *was* fine, most of the time, but the lapses in understanding continued and eventually I had to take my head out of the sand. When I disclosed my worries to our family doctor, a supportive man who had seen us through all sorts of crises, he didn't dismiss them but referred us to the gerontology department of our local hospital so that David could undergo tests.

The initial tests were the crudest you can imagine. We were ushered into a sort of long hall, one side of which was lined with small cubicles. Inside these cubicles old men (I saw no women), deaf for the most part, answered questions put to them by junior doctors. Or didn't.

It went something like this:

Who is the President of Ireland?

What?

What city are we in?

What?

What day of the week is it?

What?

The doctors shouted at the old men, who shouted back.

David passed the test with flying colours. He knew who the President was; he knew what day of the week it was. Surely there must be some other tests he could undergo? Sure enough, when a doctor saw him later on and talked to him and gave him shapes to look at and name, he told me what I already knew: David was in the early stages of dementia, a progressive disease for which there was no cure.

There is a psychological difference between suspecting something and suddenly knowing it to be true. I wasn't particularly upset but I began to live my life differently. For the first time since childhood, I began to live in the present; the future was somewhere I didn't want to go. There were no dramatic changes. David continued to search for talent but now, from time to time, he would ask me for help with his correspondence. He was having difficulty typing and his handwriting was becoming smaller and smaller and more indecipherable so I offered to type his letters for him.

I don't know if he thought there was anything wrong with him: certainly, he behaved as if he didn't. The only acknowledgement he made was that he would tell friends who called that his memory had got very bad. His difficulties in understanding what was said to him didn't seem to increase but I began to notice small changes in his personality, the sort of changes I would never have expected. He had always been anti-social but suddenly he wanted to accept every invitation that fell through our letterbox – poetry readings, novel launches, lectures. When he got to these events he talked. If he saw a writer he would make a beeline for them, usually beginning with, 'I was going to drop you a line...'

This change might be considered a good thing – that, at this late stage David was becoming more engaged with life. It should have pleased me that he was easy enough in himself to be able to approach people freely, such a change from his earlier, shyer self. But there was something wrong with the way he greeted people and I could often see that they thought so too. There is always a restraint in human intercourse and David could seem overpowering now, especially with someone who was an acquaintance rather than a friend.

I also saw a shift in power that I found upsetting. In the old days, when David, with reluctance, attended a party or launch he would stand somewhere at the back of the room and people would approach him. His shyness held him back but writers, young and old, wanted to talk to him. Now, he seemed to be making the running and the writers were backing off. I thought I might have been imagining this because I had become protective of him but I don't think this was the case.

Luckily David saw none of this. He was happy most of the time although, occasionally, he seemed to sense that there was something wrong. Momentarily he would look confused, then upset, but this never lasted long and he was back to his busyness, reading or dropping some writer a line.

I knew that this was a temporary slowing down of the disease but it was one we both benefited from so I refused to think of what lay ahead. Life wasn't all glum and Sarah's regular visits home were something we both enjoyed. It was lovely to see the love between father and daughter and the pleasure each could still take in the other's company, sitting together in silence or listening to music.

– Twenty-one –

When Sarah had been in London for a few years she began to talk about a boyfriend, someone who had become important in her life and whom she'd like to bring home some weekend. The relationship was in the early stages, she said, but she thought she liked him and she wanted him to see the city where she had been born and brought up as much as she wanted him to meet us.

Tom was a delightful young Englishman, tall and funny and obviously in love with Sarah. My only reservation was his nationality, not on any racial grounds but because if the relationship were to become serious and they eventually married they were likely to settle in London rather than Dublin.

On the second evening of their visit we all went out to dinner. As we were putting on our coats David called Tom aside and told Sarah and me to go on ahead. As we walked to the restaurant Sarah and I joked that David was probably asking Tom if his intentions were honourable. We weren't far off the mark. What David said, Tom told us later, was that he was giving them his blessing – he would welcome him as a son-in-law.

We laughed about it but I saw some of the old David in what he had done. He was looking out for his daughter and giving a bit of encouragement to a young man he regarded as an acceptable partner.

When Sarah and Tom had returned to London and we were alone again I became more aware of the dementia. It had become more than a word or a diagnosis and was a reality that had come to live with us, although its presence was still quite discreet. David still managed to live a semi-autonomous life, going up and down to Rathmines, keeping in touch with writers, even putting on the odd bet. We talked more than we had done in years and life seemed to be jogging along nicely. I thought that we could both live with this level of his condition: I just had to be more alert and avoid certain situations or foresee a circumstance that would affect David and knock him off balance.

Then he was admitted to hospital for a minor procedure, to be discharged within days. I noticed, after he had recovered from the procedure and should have been looking forward to going home, that he seemed to have become much more confused. He didn't know where he was or what day of the week it was and he had begun to think that I was his mother. His dementia, which up until now was really only noticeable if you lived with him, was suddenly apparent to everyone. I asked one of the doctors if this would improve when he was back in his own environment and he said it might but that it was not possible to predict.

In illness, we want our doctors to be gods. We want them to be able to see into the future and tell us what to expect, whereas all they can offer us is an educated guess. At least the doctor I spoke to was honest.

David returned home but didn't grow any less confused. I realised that he couldn't be left alone when, one day not long afterwards, I had a phone call from Rathmines Garda Station to tell me that my husband was there. While I was preparing dinner in the kitchen downstairs, David had left the house and a young woman found him wandering up a laneway off Rathgar Road. She sensed that something was wrong and when she approached him he said he was going home to Cork to visit his mother. She persuaded him to get into her car and took him to the Garda station.

What I remember most clearly about that incident was the

way the Gardaí looked at me and watched my reactions when I was reunited with David. They talked to David – 'Now you see, here she is, you'll be home soon' – but they were looking at me, studying my expression and how I handled David physically. Afterwards, I realised that they were on the look-out for any signs of elder abuse: maybe my husband had been running away from me because I was ill-treating him. My respect for the Gardaí increased.

We went home and ate our dinner and from then on the front door was double-locked.

Soon after this incident David began to fall into rages. Before going into hospital he would get angry from time to time but this was different. Now he would suddenly stand up, looking distressed, and begin to shout about something. If I tried to calm him down he became angrier and if I said nothing this infuriated him too. He would storm around the house, shouting incoherently, and I learned that the only thing to do was leave the room, walk into the garden and disappear from his sight. I'd keep an eye on him, of course, and when I returned he would have calmed down. One evening after an episode of this kind he turned to me and said, 'I'm so glad you're back, my darling. There was an awful woman here a few minutes ago.' It would have been funny if it were not so heartbreaking.

On another occasion, he finally wore himself out after he had been rampaging around the house and Sarah and I got him to bed. She lay down beside him and as she emitted a long, heartfelt sigh he turned to her and said, 'What's the matter, my love?'

The old David, kind and gentle, was in there somewhere.

We had still been going out to dinner occasionally, something we had both enjoyed during our married life, but I found that this was no longer possible. The whole business of ordering food and waiting for it to arrive was too much for David and would set him off. We managed lunch the odd time: I would have a bowl of soup and he would have a cup of coffee and two of the gooiest pastries on offer. But anger was never far away and I had to be careful about social outings. He was such a gentle person, with so little aggression in his make-up, that this aspect of his dementia was a mystery. Where was all the anger coming from? Had it always been there, latent?

As it turned out, it was only a stage in the progress of the disease. Soon his new-found loquacity began to diminish and with it his anger. He became more and more silent and eventually stopped talking, except to answer a question put to him. This was sad because I could see him retreating from me; it was not, however, a bad stage for David. He wasn't in pain, he still enjoyed his food, he seemed happy enough. On the whole, I am grateful that he was taken by dementia rather than cancer or even heart disease because the great thing was that he didn't know he was ill, diminishing, slowly dying. Given his obsessive fear of death, this was a tremendous blessing.

Living in London but coming home regularly, Sarah could see the changes taking place in David, probably even more clearly than I could. By now she and Tom had become engaged and as they both wanted David to be at the wedding they settled on a date and everything was arranged quickly. They chose the Unitarian Church on St Stephen's Green, where the celebrant, Sarah Smith, welcomed the atheist and the Anglican and joined them in Holy Matrimony.

Looking back, I am still surprised by how joyful that day was for all of us, maybe even for David. He was by then much more advanced in his dementia but managed to sit through the ceremony, having walked his daughter up the aisle. We did this together and I was grateful for the shortness of the journey as we shuffled our way forwards.

As we sat and watched the ceremony David grew restive. He had been through a lot that day, starting in the early morning when we had sheltered from the rain in the doorway of a barber's shop in Rathmines, waiting for it to open. Then he had been bundled into his good suit and more or less ignored while I fussed over Sarah. When she was dressed and ready and standing in front of us, I wished he was well enough to realise how beautiful she was but then, I asked myself, what difference did it make? He was always quite sure that he was married to the most beautiful woman in the world and the father of the most beautiful daughter.

The bride and groom lit candles and David asked me what we were doing there. He half-stood up. The ceremony was finishing, others guests had begun to move and I knew he had almost had enough. However he managed to come to the first part of the reception. I wheeled him in his wheelchair among the guests and people stopped to congratulate him, bending over him, acknowledging him as the father of the bride. Soon, it became apparent that the noise and the crowd were beginning to upset him so Louis drove him home, where Galina was waiting to put him to bed. But he had given his daughter away, he had sat through her marriage ceremony, he had been present at the important moments.

The next day all the out-of-town guests came to our house for lunch. Tom and Sarah were busy making sandwiches but I had been too distracted to think about lunch. I left them to it and took David for a drive to the Phoenix Park and we had our own sandwiches in the little café there. As we sat looking out at the rain dripping from the trees I acknowledged for the first time the reality of our new life. There would be just the two of us from now on and David was beginning to recede as the disease took hold. Soon enough there would be just one.

The disease was also beginning to take its toll in a physical way. David was finding it difficult to walk, even though he had no arthritis or any painful condition that would explain his diminishing mobility. He was also finding it difficult to get dressed in the mornings. So we established a new regime: I started to bring him breakfast in bed.

When we were first married he hated the idea of breakfast in bed but eventually I wooed him down the path of dalliance and on Sundays I'd bring a tray of coffee and croissants back to bed and we would linger there until noon. This continued until the arrival of our daughter and had been one of our great mutual pleasures.

Now the menu was curtailed: every morning David had an orange followed by brown bread with marmalade. He had avoided brown bread all his life but now there was no choice. I felt bad about denying him white bread but he had to have roughage. I did make sure that his coffee was strong, hot and sweet, the way he liked it.

After breakfast I'd help him to get dressed, then he would sit in the sitting room, reading *The Irish Times*. I don't know if he understood anything of what he read but he turned the pages and was happy to sit there until lunchtime, after which we headed out for a drive.

My little car became our new resource. In the beginning we went to the sea or the mountains, where I would find somewhere to stop and look out, but after a while we began to go to the Phoenix Park and, increasingly, we returned to it. I love that park – it is so large with so much activity going on. I would drive up one road and down another. Sometimes we'd stop to look at a football match or at a group of runners; always we sought out the deer. In the summer we bought ice-cream cones and licked them as we watched little children playing or lovers strolling under the trees. David relaxed there in a way he had never done when we were in the mountains or by the sea. It was urban and enclosed and I think he found this reassuring.

But the disease was marching inexorably onwards, eating into his brain. He was having difficulty with his coordination and a physiotherapist we visited suggested that I start throwing a ball to him for him to try to return it to me. I thought this would appeal to the sportsman in him and it did, except that on the second day he fell and couldn't get up and I couldn't lift him. I called the fire brigade, the first of many summonses as it turned out. The team

– big, handsome young men – carried him up to his bed. He fell several times after that, usually at night, when he was trying to get out of bed to 'spend a penny' as he put it, before I realised what was happening.

The fire engines must, eventually, have known their way to our door and the firemen who arrived in the cold, dark hours of the night were unfailingly courteous and good-humoured. Throughout the years of David's decline I found myself relying, like Blanche DuBois, on the kindness of strangers.

But I don't want this to be a cosy book with the picture of a devoted wife patiently looking after her husband. I was far more demented than devoted. There were times I shouted at David, when I had to restrain myself from hitting him. There is nothing easy about looking after someone with dementia and I was a bad-tempered woman with a short fuse and a husband who required more and more minding. He became incontinent and needed help eating. What about a nursing home, someone suggested.

My first ignoble thought was: could we afford it? At that time, nursing homes in Dublin cost more than a thousand euro a week and although David was failing mentally he was still physically fine and could live for several years. What would happen when our savings ran out? Would I have to sell our house?

I dithered, wondering what to do, but my mind was made up after a weekend that he spent in a nursing home, as respite for me. It was the first time we had tried this and the nursing home seemed excellent. When we walked in he was hailed by his old friend, the poet Basil Payne. Basil, an established resident, was suffering from dementia too but he recognised David immediately. David, however, failed to recognise him.

At this stage, one would have said that it wouldn't matter to David where he was living as long as he was looked after but although he mightn't have known that I was his wife, he knew that I was not a stranger. I saw the expression of panic in his eyes as I left him and the gratitude and relief when I went to take him home.

Even though he couldn't express any of this, either his fear or his relief, I knew then that I simply couldn't leave him in a nursing home on a long-term basis. But if I were to keep him at home I had to put certain provisions in place. Minding someone on a daily basis isn't easy and by then I could see that I needed regular time off in order to keep going. I would have to arrange to have someone else to look after David during these periods but it had to be someone who knew how to deal with a person who had dementia.

I found that the Alzheimer's Society was a great resource. They offered trained care assistants who would come to the house and stay with David for an hour or two to give me a break. David didn't respond to most of them, which made it more difficult for me. There was, however, one young man to whom he really took a shine. He was from Mauritius, a gentle, good-looking boy who kissed David on the cheek when he arrived and before he left. I think David could sense the warmth emanating from this boy, the natural respect he showed him when they met.

Carer is a new word in our vocabularies as we live longer and family structures change. But it is an apposite word, for that is exactly what the person does – he or she cares and looks after someone you love and, by extension, cares for you. Carers are undervalued in our society, both the voluntary and the paid. A good carer has to have empathy, intelligence and imagination as well as being fundamentally kind. I think I lack the natural kindness to be a good carer but I could recognise it when I saw it in that young man from Mauritius.

Another great carer was Galina from Belarus, whom I met independently of the Alzheimer's Society. She was immensely capable, the mother of a teenage boy, and able to deal effectively but gently with David's rages. When she was around she made me feel that I wasn't alone.

During this time Louis visited David every week and took him out to lunch somewhere nearby. I think what Louis found most difficult was the fact that his brother had more or less stopped speaking. But David's temporary loquacity had been out of character. He had always been a man of few words and now, in his dementia, this tendency was reaching a logical conclusion.

Apart from that we had few visitors. Dementia is an isolating condition for it must seem that there is little point in visiting someone who doesn't recognise you and who doesn't respond to you in any way. Friends tried. Vincent and Róisín Banville suggested that he might like to have lunch in the Lord Edward and it might be possible if I went with him. They collected us and everything was fine until we were seated in the restaurant, when David got upset and began to show signs of aggression. We left and walked around the corner to a taxi rank. Once we were alone together he grew calm again.

It was better if we went to friends' houses: David was more relaxed and the friends understood his confusion and helped him. But he got little pleasure from such outings and I became tenser as the meal wore on so, in the end, it seemed easier to stay at home.

The idea of having the carers in was to allow me to have time to myself, which is what I thought I needed. I didn't like leaving David at night and anyway I was usually tired: so my free time was in the afternoons. I had imagined myself going to the cinema or visiting exhibitions but now what I longed for was company. I spent most of my time virtually alone, so going out somewhere and spending more time alone was not appealing. In the past this would not have bothered me but now I began to feel isolated, wandering around aimlessly. I was reminded of the time when Sarah was a baby and I had felt that same sense of isolation: but then she had been growing towards speech and understanding, the reverse of what was now happening to her father.

I no longer looked forward to the arrival of the carers. I remember one particularly bleak outing, a Sunday afternoon when the wind was blowing in from the Irish Sea and the skies were low and grey. I wandered into town, stopped on one of the bridges over the Liffey and looked down at the brown, sluggish water. I was cold and miserable and the world around me reflected my misery back to me. In O'Connell Street I went into Clery's café, a place I had never been before. It was full of mammies and children and women friends sharing pots of tea. I ran out of the place without ordering anything. This was the first time my loneliness crystallised for me. I also realised that it was David I was missing, not my friends. He was essentially gone and I knew I was not going to get him back. The word 'desolation' was what came to me to express my feeling of sadness and hopelessness.

However, most of the time, I was too busy for much reflection. I got a wheelchair from the HSE and a disabled sticker for my car. I discovered that the National Concert Hall was wheelchair friendly and I started taking David to lunchtime concerts. The wheelchairs are positioned at the back of the auditorium so if David became unhappy it was easy enough to wheel him out. But on the whole he seemed to enjoy these short concerts. With disabled parking just outside and a ramp at the entrance it was a very easy outing.

That laminated square of blue cardboard on my windscreen made my life much easier. I could go into town with David, park in a disabled bay and wander round the shops with him. Perhaps it was a meaningless outing for both of us but at least it was an outing. The city council has provided plenty of disabled parking bays and, on the whole, they are not abused. I found that the exception to this was supermarket car parks. For some reason or another some shoppers seem to think that it is all right to park in a disabled bay if they are only going to be a few minutes. When I came across such offenders I would confront them. To my surprise they appeared to be normal, civilised people – much chastened by the time I had finished with them. I still confront such offenders if I see them leaving a car without a sticker in a disabled bay. As David used to say after he had remonstrated with someone for bad behaviour: 'They have to learn.'

David and I continued to go for our afternoon drives to the

Phoenix Park. Now I played a CD or turned on the radio as there was no longer any talking between us. One evening on the way home another driver cut in front of me and I started to swear. To my amazement, David began to laugh with genuine amusement and after that there were many deliberate swearing sessions in the car. They caused David great amusement and the sound of his laughter was a happy sound.

We are, as a nation, pretty foul-mouthed but neither David nor I ever swore or cursed. The use of bad language was one of the first changes I saw in David and now I too had begun to use it. When our daughter became a teenager I remember how distressed I was to hear ugly words coming out of her mouth – a phase that, thankfully, lasted only a short time. Now, when she came home on a visit I found myself watching my language. But a habit is hard to break and she reprimanded me on more than one occasion. I have weaned myself off the habit, I think, but I still have visions of myself descending on her English in-laws, swearing and holding out my glass for a refill, the walking embodiment of the stereotypical Irish mother-in-law.

Before the onset of his dementia, the only time I ever heard David use bad language was also while driving. When we married, he could not drive. He was nearly fifty at the time but I was determined that I was not going to spend the rest of our married lives driving him around, especially as I was the drinker in the family. So I bullied him into learning and, to my astonishment, he turned out to be a natural, passing his test the first time.

Once behind the wheel, he underwent a change of personality. Usually cautious, he drove too fast for my liking and was quite aggressive, shouting at other drivers to get out of the way and, on occasion, using a rich selection of four-letter words. It was like watching Dr Jekyll turning into Mr Hyde. I began to offer to drive and he didn't seem to mind, so eventually we returned to the old regime and David let his driving licence lapse.

– Twenty-two –

It was coming up to five years since David had begun to show the initial signs of dementia. What surprised me about the disease was how badly it affected him physically, although, if you think that every physical movement we make has been prompted by a message to the brain, it makes complete sense. David was becoming more disabled in general. He now had to be dressed and undressed and he could walk only with great difficulty and only if I was holding on to him. He had stopped pretending to read *The Irish Times* and simply sat in his chair, passively and calmly. He didn't seem to be in distress and his essential personality hadn't really changed as the rages had abated – with some exceptions.

The Alzheimer's Society has a house in Ranelagh where they organise activities and I took him along to a singsong they were having. Everyone sat in a semi-circle and someone began to play the piano and belt out some song. David looked around at the men and women singing along, some clapping their hands, one or two just staring vacantly. He stood up suddenly, overturning his chair and making a determined effort to escape. I took him home and never repeated the experiment. Later that evening I thought how stupid the idea had been. David was still David and of course he would hate the idea of sitting in a room with ten strangers listening to them singing out of tune. It taught me a useful lesson: he might be losing his mind but his core, his essence, was still intact.

But he had gone from me. Now the only communication

I had was when he laughed at my deliberate swearing sessions in the car. He didn't talk at all, not even yes or no, and I wondered if he was able to. I didn't go near doctors because at that time there was nothing that could be done for dementia – there probably still isn't. At one point I had read about a new drug, Aricept, that was supposed to be of some help, and I asked our doctor to prescribe it. It made no noticeable difference to David and swallowing it caused him distress so I abandoned the experiment.

Although the days might have been long they were so filled with doing things that they passed quickly. The nights were worse because there was always the possibility that David would get out of bed before I realised it and end up falling. I have never been a good sleeper but with this extra anxiety I hardly slept at all. I was exhausted but, as new parents quickly find out, one can get by on little sleep.

Then there were moments of intense happiness. I remember one day when I had a free afternoon walking around the lake in Bushy Park. I stopped to watch the ducks fighting over scraps of bread. The sun was unseasonably warm, the sky was high and blue, the ducks and the children feeding them were having fun – and so was I. I saw that there had been other times in my life when I had been much more cast down. When I stopped to analyse my feelings I found an easy explanation: because there was no future I had learned to live in the present. The park, the ducks, the sun, it was as good as it got – not only that, it was good enough.

I walked home trying to hold on to that feeling but of course it didn't last. Nevertheless it helped me: in some way the ducks and the sunshine and the children became a counterpoint to the shrinking world I now inhabited with someone who had been my husband.

– Twenty-three –

The status quo could have gone on for months, even years; although David was much feebler his heart was still beating strongly. He was still eating regularly, although his appetite had diminished. I didn't really think about what would happen, dealing with each day as it came, concentrating on my tasks, less anxious than I had been at many periods of my life.

Then one morning after I had got David up and dressed and sitting in his usual chair he suddenly slumped sideways. I straightened him up but he slumped again and I saw that he was unconscious. Pushing his chair against the wall so that he wouldn't fall on the floor I went to phone for an ambulance. He was taken to the accident and emergency department of St James's Hospital where he was quickly assessed, then admitted to a ward of noise and bedlam with each patient looking at an individual television set. It made no difference to David, the man who had loved quiet. He had regained consciousness on the journey to the hospital but kept his eyes closed and didn't respond as I talked and held his hand. As I looked at him in the hospital bed, in a blue hospital gown, he seemed to have shrunk and taken several steps closer to death.

After about a week he was moved to a four-bedded ward. The three men with whom he shared it were also suffering from dementia and were more or less the same age as him. They were to become his final companions. He had had another bleed into the brain; we were entering the home straight.

You could say that those four men were bed-blockers because I don't think any of them was having much medical treatment. But this was before Mary Harney's 'Fair Deal' and if one could keep a relative in hospital and out of a nursing home one did.

I felt the same, initially, but then I began to feel guilty about David taking up a bed in an acute hospital. I knew that at this stage it really didn't make any difference to him where he was so I started looking into nursing homes. The problem was that David now needed nursing care and although I saw many good places none of them could complete with the care given by St James's. As well as doctors there were nurses, care assistants, physiotherapists, speech therapists – a whole bevy of professionals to look after patients. Hospitals are in a different league from nursing homes and cost millions more to run – as we would all know if we spent time in hospital without any kind of subvention.

So my efforts to find a nursing home were half-hearted and the pressure the hospital put on me to do so was always gentle and considerate. I could see that David was failing physically: he wouldn't be a bed-blocker for too long.

A year ago I went back to St James's to see a consultant. I had been dreading it, driving my car into that familiar car park and getting the lift up to the concourse with its bustle and colour. I feared being returned to those days when the hospital had become a home-from-home for me.

My experience was quite the reverse. I felt a calmness, a loosening of tension as I waited to ask for directions at the reception desk. This was the hospital where David had died, where I had watched him grow thinner and weaker by the day. But none of this came back to me then. What I was remembering was the all-encompassing care and love he had received – we had both received – in this hospital.

David moved further and further away. He had stopped talking for some time before being admitted to hospital and now he seemed completely cut off from the outside world. He didn't really react when I came in to see him; he would stare at my face but his expression of puzzlement never changed. His reaction to all his visitors was the same and I was almost sure that by now he could not tell one person from another. Yet, as I watched him, I saw this expression change when a nurse or care assistant approached, to be replaced by one of fear. He didn't seem to know me or Sarah or Louis; yet, at some level, he seemed to recognise that we were familiar, while the hospital personnel were strangers.

At such moments I wondered if I should try to bring him home but in reality I knew that there was no question of it. He had to be washed and fed and lifted in and out of bed, a task that needed a minimum of two strong people. As I lay in bed at night I would come up with impossible plans, calculating how long our savings would last with round-the-clock care for him at home.

Then another problem arose. Peter, one of the old men, who was ambulant, would get himself out of bed, belt up in his dressing gown and stand at the end of David's bed, staring down at him. He was a small, bantam-like chap and there was nothing threatening about him but his behaviour obviously distressed David. There was nothing to be done. When I went in, I'd move him gently away and stand where he had been standing but I wasn't there all the time. The staff would suggest he move but he ignored them and they could hardly tie him to his bed. I thought of asking if I could have David moved to another ward but eventually the other man lost interest in him and left him alone.

I tried to visit him every day and every day as I walked home I wondered how long he would live. I couldn't say that I wanted him to die but I didn't want him to live, either – not as he was. His heart and lungs were still strong. I began to revise my opinion and to think that this might be a long goodbye. But the disease moved forward inexorably. He began to refuse his food. At first I tried feeding him and when that didn't work I started bringing him food from home, things I knew he liked. But nothing seemed to appeal to him: he couldn't be tempted even by sugar and he grew quite gaunt. His poor arms, emerging from the sleeves of his pyjamas, were like sparrows' legs.

I bought a little portable CD player and when I visited him I played him Mozart – sunny, happy Mozart. I also read his own poems to him, written when he was a young man and reissued in a slim volume some years previously. Before I left him, I always brought my face close to his and said, 'I love you very much, David, and I'll see you tomorrow'. As I watched his eyes, I thought I saw fear and was very aware as I walked out the door that I was leaving him to the care of strangers.

As time passed by, I did want him to die. He was getting thinner and thinner; he seemed frightened and maybe in pain; he was not going to get any better. I was afraid that the hospital would start feeding him through a tube and I thought of the extra discomfort that would cause him. I walked to and from the hospital every day and at night I slept, in a suspended state now as life continued on around me.

David had very faithful visitors during those months in hospital – I remember especially his brother, Louis, and his friend, Tony Glavin. Some good friends found it more difficult or even frightening and didn't repeat an initial visit.

It was difficult to visit him, even for me. He lay in bed, his bones visible through a gossamer-thin skin. His eyes were enlarged and staring, frightened. But his strong heart kept beating and his lungs kept drawing in the warm hospital air.

I settled into a rhythm of hospital visits bookended by long walks. It seemed as if this could go on for many months. And then, when I was least expecting it, I got that call from the hospital. David was beginning to fail; I should summon any family members who lived abroad.

I phoned Sarah and went into the hospital. David's eyes were closed now and his breathing audible. I sat and prepared to wait. I knew the drill as I had been through it with my parents, who had both died within a fortnight of each other in Doctor Steevens' Hospital. I was familiar with hospitals at night time when patients have been sedated into sleep and the lights are dimmed and the nurses' station forms an oasis of life and warmth at the end of the ward. They are eerie places but there is something tranquil about them too.

The next morning Sarah arrived and we sat with David throughout the day and night, taking turns to go out and get something to eat. Towards dawn, a nurse suggested that one or other of us go home and get some rest but neither of us wanted to move until the sun was properly up in the sky. As a species we may have conquered darkness but not our atavistic fear of it. Everything somehow seems better, more hopeful, once the sun is up.

As it turned out, our wait was not to be long. David died at the next dawn, signalling his departure with a strange, guttural sound as if the heart, the spirit, was escaping from the diminished body. We said goodbye and kissed his already cooling forehead. All his life he had raged against the dying of the light but that light was now, after eighty-four years, finally extinguished.

We left the ward that had in some senses become a second home for me. Down below we met the consultant and signed papers and thanked various people for the care they had given David over the previous six months.

It was a beautiful May morning. By then Tom had arrived and the three of us went for a walk out into Dublin port along the length of the South Wall. The sun was shining on the water and seagulls swooped. The pulse of life was strong everywhere and I could only be glad that David's sufferings were over. I looked around me, out towards Wicklow where the mountains were visible, backlit by an early-summer sun, and I thought, as I often do, how beautiful this world is. Nothing made much sense but the world was still beautiful.

– Afterwards –

David has been dead for almost seven years and in many ways I am quite the merry widow. I do things and go places; I enjoy spending time with my family and friends. Life is changed in that I now live alone, something I never did before, and which I have discovered I enjoy. I am free to please myself. Yet I know that this is not the whole story.

Immediately after David's death I felt a huge relief. His sufferings were over and I didn't have to worry about him any longer. His funeral service, conducted by Sarah Smith, was secular, with a pianist playing that Mozart piece he had practised every day, poetry and the shared memories of friends. We gave him a good send-off.

When life returned to the quotidian, I don't remember feeling anything much. If this was grief it was an absence of emotion rather than any overwhelming feelings. Perhaps it was in an effort to feel something that, a few months after David's death, I took myself off to Mount Melleray where the monks have a guesthouse. The monastery is situated in the Golden Vale, that lovely, under-appreciated world of rich rolling countryside and distant blue hills. There are no houses visible from the grounds and in the fields around fat, happy cows look up from their munching to stare at you with mild brown eyes.

Although I hadn't intended this as a religious retreat I went to vespers that first evening and watched the white-clothed, white-headed monks file into the chapel. I listened to their chanting voices, heightened in register by age. Outside the sun moved through the sky, casting shadows on the walls.

I got up in time for matins the next morning and spent the day in silence, realising, suddenly, the greater silence all around. I felt I could become a permanent resident for there was nothing calling me back to Dublin and there was something very seductive about this retired, silent world.

When I returned home I fell into a state of ennui – it seems an affected word but it is the only one that fits. Nothing much seemed to touch me. I ate, I slept, I accepted invitations. In my house I made permanent changes, moving to a small back bedroom and changing my sitting room to what had been David's study. I told myself I was making these changes for practical reasons as it would be much cheaper to heat only the bottom half of the house.

Then, suddenly, I developed a dreadful itch. My limbs, my trunk, my head – all felt as if something were crawling over them. I went to various doctors, was prescribed antihistamines and, later, steroids, went on a variety of diets and changed my washing powder. Nothing made any difference. I was driven demented but the itch persisted and the doctors could offer no explanation. It disappeared as mysteriously as it had arrived, I don't even know precisely when, but while it was raging I had no thought for anything else. It occupied me completely.

I returned to feeling nothing much. People who met me told me I was looking well; friends told me I was great. I knew what they meant: I slapped on the make-up in the morning and didn't break down when I met someone for coffee. I was coping, they surmised.

But coping suggests that there is some effort involved, whereas I was feeling nothing. I wasn't sad, I wasn't lonely. I was busy or happily idle. Sometimes, when someone enquired, 'How are you doing?' I'd nod and smile, conveying, I hoped, that I was indeed coping because what I was experiencing was so much harder to convey.

At the end of the summer I went to Ronda in the south of Spain. One of Sarah's friends had a flat there and offered it to me for an extended stay. En route, in Malaga bus station, one of my bags was stolen and I was sans passport, money, credit cards and laptop. Juan in the ticket office rescued me. When he heard my tale of woe, he brought me home to his wife and after we'd had dinner these two kind people drove me up to Ronda. I had a roof over my head and a jar of instant coffee in the kitchen. The following day money would be wired to me through Western Union and eventually the Irish embassy would sort out travel documents. I watched myself with detached interest, as if the whole thing were happening to someone else.

There were two flats in the house, both on the upper floor, one permanently unoccupied. On the ground floor there was a number of empty store rooms and on the roof a large terrace. There was no natural light in the stairway or landings and the electric light, on a timer, often cut out before I reached the door of my flat.

The flat itself was lovely but the house had a spooky feeling, especially as most of it was empty. Yet from the first night I found myself sleeping much better than was normal for me. For the first six weeks I spoke to nobody, apart from the butcher next door and the fishmonger. I spent hours under an awning on the roof terrace in the deadening heat. When it grew cooler I went for walks through the town and out past the gorge for which Ronda is famous. I took a bus trip to Seville and another to Algatocín, a small town further up in the mountains.

When I spent time in Spain as a student and later as a young teacher, I had always been aware of myself as a foreigner. I had stood out, with my pale skin and red hair; sometimes I was admired and sometimes derided as just odd looking. Now I wasn't noticed no matter where I went. I had become invisible, as women do when they go beyond a certain age. This must also have been true at home but it was in Spain that I first became aware of it and I found it liberating rather than insulting. I could wander at will, just another ageing woman.

I didn't do much conscious thinking but when I tried to think about David he kept slipping away. I would put my hands out to capture his image but it flowed through my fingers like water. He would not stay still for long enough for me to get hold of him.

It took me a while to realise that he wasn't backing away from me but that I was backing away from him. In shame. Shame has been my default mode all my life and now this shame had something to latch on to: my inadequacies as a wife, my selfishness, the many times when I had been brusque instead of tender, impatient instead of caring.

No wonder I had been feeling so little emotion. Had I ever really loved David? This thought came to me as I sat on the terrace in the early afternoon when all Ronda seemed either to be asleep or dead. The brightness of the light was intensified by the white walls of the terrace and I stared at this blankness, listening to the deafening beat of my heart.

The next day I signed on for a summer language course and found myself among American students, years younger than Sarah. Their chatter about bars and parties and who was sleeping with whom helped to damp down my feelings of panic.

I would not spend any more long afternoons on that terrace, pinned down by the whiteness and the heat with no escape from my thoughts. I would listen to the teacher and struggle with the subjunctive and do my homework, filling my days with structure, giving myself no time to stray into the danger of remembrance.

After some months I was glad to get home to my house and Zena the cat. We had got her from a neighbour shortly after Vashti died and we named her after the tennis player Zena Garrison because, like Garrison, she was black and wiggled her hips. She was elderly by now, sleeping most of the day. In the evenings she would jump on to my lap and sleep there for an hour or two before she headed out through the cat flap to do whatever it is that cats do at night. I didn't pay her any more attention than she paid me but she was company: I realised this when I got home from Ronda and there she was, waiting for me in the hall.

Then one day, some months later, she went off her food. She began to ail and when I took her to the vet he said that she had a tumour. He didn't recommend an operation because of her age. I held her while he administered the lethal injection and then I took her home. I would bury her in the garden, where Vashti had been buried. David had dug Vashti's grave and I found it very difficult to dig as deeply as the vet advised. I did the best I could, placed Zena's now stiff body, wrapped in her blanket, in the bottom of the hole, filled in the earth and put the spade away.

As I was washing my hands I began to cry and once I started it seemed as if I couldn't stop. I sat and let the tears flow, making no effort to staunch them. Here was the grief I hadn't felt when David died. I remembered that we had got the cat as a tiny kitten, how she had hid under a sofa for the first day, how at first we had thought her inferior to the aristocratic Vashti and had then grown to love her for herself. She had been part of a life that was over – a husband, a daughter, a cat.

I cried until my body ached and I was hollowed out. Zena was dead.

The next morning when I woke I lay for some seconds before I remembered what had happened: when I did the waves of sorrow began to flow over me again. I was alone now, definitively alone. Zena was dead and I would never have another cat.

I can't remember how long this crazy, skewed thinking continued but at some stage, as I continued to mourn my cat, the recurring image of me in the garden, digging, preparing Zena's grave, became jumbled up with Vashti's grave and it was David who was doing the digging. He had come back to me and I could hear him say, 'Crumbs', his strongest expletive, as earth fell back into the hole. I saw bits of him but odd bits, like the pores in his nose and the cuticles of his square, small nails.

When I went to the kitchen to make myself a cup of tea he came with me. I remembered how he had always called me, 'My love.'

And that's what I was. He was mine too. I had loved him, in my fashion and imperfectly, but I had loved him.

I felt a sudden dismay that he was gone. Over the coming days I began to remember the things we had done together, the events of our lives, how, although I was the bossy one he was the one who had always looked after me. This was the David I had forgotten.

But now I would not let him linger, for that told only part of the story. This was not the David who had died: time and illness had changed him into the poor, depleted husband who sat silently in his chair, unable to make sense of the newspaper on his lap.

It was good that his sufferings were over; it was good that David was no more.

Later, before Christmas, when the snows came, hungry foxes dug Zena's skeleton up. I watched them through the window, thinking at first that they were just playing, but when I went to investigate I found her tiny skull.

Alas poor Yorick. I felt a sudden consolation: this is what we would all come to, our common end. This has been my consolation since then, not in any nihilistic way but accepting the naturalness of death. It is more a question of 'Gather ye rosebuds' than 'Rage, rage against the dying of the light'.

David is gone but his death was not a tragedy. He lived a long and fulfilled life and he has left an inestimable legacy, on the pinnacle of which sit the two little grandchildren he has never seen.

He was an editor, he was a husband, he was a father.

He was a man, take him for all in all.

And I loved him.